WATER FOR THE SOUL

A Father's Hope For His Son

Michael Tyler

ISBN: 1-4033-5697-1 (e-book)
ISBN: 1-4033-5698-X (Paperback)
ISBN: 1-4033-5699-8 (Dust Jacket)

Library of Congress Control Number: 2002093517

This book is printed on acid free paper.

Printed in the United States of America
Bloomington, IN

1stBooks - rev. 4/14/03

Dedication

To my son, Sascha —
Though a single cloud can block the light of the sun,
it can never stop it from shining.
Such is my love for you.

In memory of my mother, Joan —
For all the lessons you gave, that I can now give.
May you live on in the giving.

CONTENTS

Preface .... **vii**
Poem: ***The Island of Resolution*** .... **ix**

Chapter 1: Baba's Pledge **1**
Chapter 2: Identity **11**
Chapter 3: Intent **19**
Chapter 4: Family **36**
Chapter 5: Spirituality **48**
Chapter 6: Perception **54**
Chapter 7: Diseases of Character **62**
Chapter 8: My Final Instruction **75**

Preface

This book began as a journal to my son, in 1994. He was only five then. I am making it available to anyone, so that someday it can be available for him to find. It is written with the transcending love known only from creating a life to love; with the unmatched elation of having fulfilled my greatest ambition by becoming his father; with the sustaining joy of memories saved from days when we were together; with the clinging hope that he will become all the glory endowed within him.

It also is written with the unremitting pain of having been estranged from him, by the animosity of divorce; with the consuming sorrow of missed memories from days that can never be recaptured; with the agonizing speculation about whether our relationship will ever resume.

As he matures and develops into his ambition, I fear the effect of my absence may cast a burdening shadow on his life. I employ my words, with the greatest expectation of duty and purpose, to offer him light into whatever cellars his psyche might descend, or tunnels that demand his exploration for self-knowledge, or darkness that prevents him from discovering the beauty of his spirit.

Additionally, may these words provide him consolation for despairing tears, guidance for an uncertain journey, resolve when doubt threatens and satiety for the hunger of his completion. But most of all, I hope these words will assure and convince him that my love, since his conception, has never been false, has never wavered, has never been abandoned and has never stopped fostering the fervent desire to be his "Papa".

I also offer this book to the many parents who, like myself, live with the agony of a divorce-induced alienation from their children. The desire for them, constant and tormenting, is your worst starvation. The disconnection, painful and depressing, is your personal plague. The regret for an unrecoverable history, haunting and immeasurable, is your lifetime scar.

I hope my words will provide you with some solace, redemption and encouragement. To whatever end they can reaffirm your parental value and effect a rejoining of broken bonds, I would urge you to use them.

You must never lose hope.
Love depends on it.

The Island of Resolution

If you venture beyond the shoreline of your anxiety,
To challenge crossing the sea of your fears,
And steer your sail with honest faith
Towards the call of your completion;
Then chance the Perfidious Horizon,
To dare the squalls that measure courage,
And command your will to brave the midnight
That preludes Morning's peace —
You will come upon a place,
Preserved by pure devotion,
Untouched by bitter winds
And cast in splendid truth;
Here is where you'll find me,
On the Island of Resolution,
Ready to make the voyage
To journey our reunion.

Baba's Pledge

I was five or six years old, when I asked my grandmother why kissing someone was called "giving them some sugar". She said because babies aren't born sweet, you have to make them that way and the only way to do that was to kiss them a lot, because a kiss is "soul sugar".

When you were born, I gave you one hundred kisses a day.

May 26, 1999

My son, today is your birthday and you are now ten years old. Since you were five, I have been writing to and for you. It was at this age that my relationship with you was critically fractured. I have seen and had very little contact with you, since.

I keep a picture of you in my wallet. You are eighteen-months old in the photo. Though I have others, I have chosen this one. When I look at it, I can reclaim a time when our relationship was intact and full of promise, a time before there was concern of it becoming the casualty of caustic emotions.

You are a constant presence in my thoughts, from my first recognition of the day to my acceptance of the night. Sometimes I recall or imagine conversations with you, to safeguard against forgetting your voice. Other times, I close my eyes and reconstruct your face. I still have an unopened piece of candy you once gave me. I count it amongst my most valued keepsakes. There are days when I revisit places we have been together, walk paths we have walked before. I often wonder what you think about and if you are thinking about me.

I was thirteen years old, when my parents divorced. In the months and years that followed, I came to realize that becoming a father was my most desired goal. At age eighteen, I discovered the word "Baba", a term used in African and Asian cultures to mean, "Father". As it was explained to me, "Baba" translates into "one who protects, preserves and promotes". It was once used as a title for African kings, as they were deemed the fathers of their nations. It is part of the message, *"Baba Ati Omo"* (Father and Child), on a necklace I gave to you at age four. I offered it as an amulet, to protect against any erosion of your sentiment for me.

"Baba" defines my role as your father. I will always seek to protect, preserve and promote you. My parental actions on your behalf are guided by this oath. Should you have a child someday, perhaps you will consider it a worthy pledge.

Also, should you become a father, heed this. Having a child is the single most selfish thing you can do, for a child doesn't ask to be born. You create life for reasons of your own desire. It is also the single most important thing you can do, for no experience can eclipse the experience that begets all others. Recognize this dual significance. From your selfish desire will come the most altruistic and abundant experience of your life, and from the importance of your child's birth will come your most humbling reality. Reconcile your desire to your child's importance and you will parent well.

Years ago when the turbulence of my divorce from your mother impacted our relationship, I decided to not engage a legal battle for resolution. I can recall speaking to you on the phone, just days before I presented that decision to the court. The distress in your voice was obvious. You spoke with an unsettling pain, the type that children sometimes suffer and parents can do nothing about. A sense of guilt emerged from your attempts to apologize for a dilemma not of your making. The tears you cried warped the steadiness of your voice. You sensed it would not be long, before what we once considered normal would be dramatically changed.

I desperately sought for some way to bring you ease. Whether I did or not I am uncertain of, but what came to mind was to sing to you, something I had often done before. The song I sang was "Don't Cry" by Seal.

You listened as I struggled to deliver the song with a tone of comfort, rather than with my own distress. Your emotions made this all the more challenging, for each tearful sigh you expressed intensified the gravity of the moment, a gravity I realized would soon exceed my capacity for spiritual resistance. With eyelids shut and tears streaming, I pressed on, desperately trying to feign the assurance parents must often provide to tame the worries of their children.

Every moment I had spent with you, until that phone call, surfaced to form a montage in my mind. Each memory dared the words in my throat to be heard. As I continued singing, I began to register an overwhelming sense of loss, as if the end of our conversation would mark the end of our relationship.

Before I finished, you hung up without saying good-bye. What followed was the most compressing silence I have ever experienced. But from the silence emerged resolution. That possibility can best be explained, by a passage I once heard. I am uncertain of the source:

> "There are definitely moments in life when silence has sound; when the incredible hush of what is physically audible allows one to hear loudly, the vocabulary of what the heart feels and what the mind remembers."

In that incredible hush, what I heard was a recollection of the Old Testament tale of King Solomon, found in I Kings 3:16-28. The story recounts his settlement of a dispute between two women, over who was the real mother of an infant boy. Upon drawing his sword to divide the child into equal halves, one of the women stepped forward to relinquish her claim, pleading that the child's life be spared. The other urged on for the division and inevitable death of the child, in order to nullify a parental claim by either of them.

King Solomon then awarded the child, to the woman who relinquished her claim. He did so reasoning that the real mother would do anything to spare her child death, even if it meant never seeing him again.

A protracted court battle would have surely severed your well-being and I would not be Solomon's sword. The fate I sought to spare you is the worst kind, a spiritual death. In that what is "spiritual" is the living essence of a thing, a spiritual death means "living" dead.

This is far more detrimental and devastating than physical death, for with the end of life comes the end of all perceivable suffering. However, a spiritual death is a continued existence of serving host to a parasitic misery that consumes all dreams, desires, appreciation, ambition, value and vitality. If not seeing you meant preventing this and giving you a chance to remain "whole", I was willing to relinquish as well.

I formally presented that decision on August 18, 1995. In so doing, I was effectively discharged from your life. I felt helpless to protect you from the situation and my lost contact meant I would not be able to promote you with praise and instruction, as I had once hoped. So I sought to satisfy the remaining directive of the "Baba pledge". I reasoned my acquiescence might preserve an environment for you, with as little hostility and upheaval as possible.

I have never deserted you. I stepped aside for the sake of your future development. I hope one day you will reason, understand and accept my decision, as I felt forced to make it. In that I would dutifully waive my fate for the potential progress of your life, I did so on that August day.

Following that decision, I experienced a pain and depression the likes of which I had not known before. I once described it to a friend, as the imagined sensation of a rat gnawing at your brain. For weeks and months to follow, I found it difficult to greet and end a day without tears. Seeing men on the street with their children would often send me into a public bathroom, grasping for composure.

I have learned to live with the heartache, much the same way one learns to live with the loss of a limb or a sense. Life is not over, but it is definitely not the same. There are many days when I still battle grief. I suspect there always will be, until we are once again united without imposition. As I await that possibility, know that my love for you has no capacity for measure.

Someday, you must make up your mind about this situation and the history it has spawned. For that reason, I will end my commentary regarding it for when that day comes, I wish to be viewed by you as an agent for clarity and not manipulation. However, in your process for resolution, I ask that you consider this predicament.

Dr. Martin Luther King Jr. once stated, "It is better to go through life with a scarred up body, rather than a scarred up soul," a comment that supports the comparison I previously made between physical and spiritual death. However, it is unfortunate that society does not equate spiritual violation with physical violation. We are more impressed by what we can immediately see, than by what takes time to be seen. Regrettably, that disparity in recognition has a condemning end for many, because protracted violation of the soul dispenses greater pain and exacts a greater toll.

Initially, my anguish was joined by an anger equal in intensity to the torment of my grief. Fortunately, I soon reasoned that I would either be engulfed by the fire of my emotions or learn to use that heat for a constructive end. Such is the case with fire. Let it burn without restraint and it will destroy all matter and air necessary to sustain itself. Learn to control it and it becomes the flame of a candle that yields light; the combustion of a furnace that yields warmth; the roast of an oven that yields food.

Since I consider parents to be the first teachers for their children, the constructive end I chose was to write down all that I had hoped to offer you, by way of instruction. Mine is a philosophical offering, an attempt to propose a value system by which you can live your life. I also desire it to be a prism for contemplation, something that will allow you to see the spectral dimensions of life. What appears to be a singular and uniform reality is actually an awe-inspiring composite of circumstances, events, perceptions, interpretations, revelations and mysteries.

As I compile this, I am writing to you with words currently beyond your years to fully comprehend. I am doing so for two reasons. First, if I can express myself as my thoughts actually formulate, I can convey the most of what I would like to say. Secondly, I have no idea if our relationship will ever resume. Should it not, perhaps one day you will come upon this text and consider its lessons, insights and perspectives to have merit beyond my parental motivation. May you take these words and judge them worthy of your use.

When I began writing, I focused on the axiom, "The force of a man will determine his rise". I believe that "force" to be the dynamism created by combining inner vision with resolve — will. With the ability to see in, you can find all that is necessary to survive, overcome, create, thrive and succeed. With resolve, you can commit yourself to achieving those ends.

I want you to have great force within your mind, body and soul. If you do, you will eclipse the combined "rise" your mother and I have individually achieved. I have always thought your potential to do so was real, for when you were born, the first words I ever spoke to you were:

"One-hundred percent of what I am is only fifty-percent of what you are. Before you become a man, you are already twice the man I will ever be."

I believe each child represents twice the endowment of his/her preceding generation, which has been compounded by every birth since the beginning of time. You are all who have gone before you and so much more. This is the esteem I will always revere you with. Let it serve as a doorway, for comprehending the bounty within you.

I have always felt it critically important for people to evaluate their lives for clear understanding, before embarking upon parenthood. You can only teach what you know and as famed child advocate Andrew Vachs has stated, "Children are a second chance to get it right."

Clear understanding is both the yield of deliberation and articulation. So I urge you to learn and respect the meaning and power of words. They are the building blocks of any information and the conduit of all communication. Nothing transacts in your mind or in the world, without words. To be effective in life, you must clearly understand what you think, say, write, hear, read and interpret. Furthermore, you must be able to completely and accurately convey your thoughts to others. Given this importance, I want you to discern the distinctions between the following words.

Information is whatever gives you awareness. Behind air and water, it is the most vital and valuable resource in the world, worth considerably more than any gold reserve imaginable. You must first know where the gold is, before you can get it.

Learning is the acquisition and processing of information, so that it becomes knowledge. It is the getting of seed, the tilling of soil, the planting of seed and the harvesting of the grain.

Knowledge is information converted into the sustenance of comprehension. If you do not understand information, it is useless. Whereas learning is the farming of grain, knowledge is the bread from which it is made. It nourishes your mind and ultimately your behavior, for thought is parent to action. You can only do what you first think to do. So pursue and consume knowledge, as you would food for your body.

Wisdom, as an axiom holds, is the knowledge of others. It is the perception, recognition and comprehension of diverse mentalities and motivations. From this type of knowledge, you can have a more effective engagement with people.

Enlightenment is the knowledge of self. It means "light brought into", which suggest that self-exploration is necessary to procure it. It is an endeavor to fully illuminate the core of your being, in order to expose and detect flaws and perfections, incompetence and skill. Once assessed, you can amend and minimize your shortcomings, while profit from and enhance your talent. Doing so will enable you to more fully perceive, effect and command your reasoning, your sentiments and your abilities. This is mastery.

Do not mistake this endeavor as an effort for greatness. Greatness is a judgment bestowed by others and history. When we are awed by Michael Jordan playing basketball, entranced by Oscar Peterson's command of the piano, charmed by Sarah Vaughn's singing and thoroughly convinced by Denzel Washington's acting, we bear testament to their mastery. They project a luminescence of ability, which can only be emitted from tapping their core. We judge them great because we recognize the rare, intense luster of their efforts. The sweat of their labor marinates our applause. Concern yourself with the labor, not the applause. Once you discover your brilliance and release its radiance, it will not be ignored.

The pursuit of enlightenment is a formidable challenge. It requires testing the tensile strength of your security line. Though many are capable, few are willing to relinquish hold of the comfort from their prescribed conditioning, to venture gain from an undefined process. As a result, you are not likely to meet many people in life with impressive and distinctive individuality. When you do, study them. Should sincere endearment and compatibility exist, befriend them, regardless of their station in life. If you pursue enlightenment, they are the people who will most understand you and few things are more frustrating, than living without being understood.

Do not fear challenge, for it stimulates all evolution — biological, sociological, technological and personal. It is the soul's excavator, forcing you to mine yourself to discover the resources that will allow you tó survive and thrive. Stored within your being is over 3.5 billion years of information, there since the first strand of DNA was constructed. All that information has persevered to enable your evolvement. Dig into it. Your inner resources are immense.

Know the difference between intelligence and judgment. **Intelligence** is the capacity to acquire and apply knowledge. **Judgment** is the capacity to form an opinion, draw a conclusion or make a decision based upon an evaluation of information. For example, President Clinton is highly intelligent, a Rhodes scholar. However, with respect to the Lewinsky scandal, his capacity for judgment seemed to be critically impaired or absent.

Accepting this distinction, recognize that "ignorance" and "stupidity" are modifiers of judgment, not intelligence. **Ignorance** is the absence of knowledge to make a sound judgment. When a child does not know the stove is hot, he might touch it and painfully gain the knowledge of injury. **Stupidity** is discretion averted. It means having the knowledge and ignoring its utility. When a woman knows her man is a lying infidel and she continues to take him back, her injury is of her own judgment.

You cannot be faulted or fault others for ignorance. When you realize it, seek to resolve yours by inquisition and that of others by your offering. Stupidity bears accountability. Make no effort to inoculate against it and it will become a disease of character that will infect your reasoning and cripple your life. Your best prevention is this three-part counsel:

1. Give attention and significance to the instruction and advice of those, whose experience exceeds yours. But scrutinize their lessons for both objective merit and rational application, lest you become an accomplice to perpetuating flawed judgment.

2. Understand that "elected ignorance" is stupidity. What I mean is that both denial and refusal are consciously and deliberately employed. Choosing not to accept, recognize or learn the truth of a situation, a person or a people does not exonerate you from the liability of your subsequent judgment.

3. Embrace your mistakes and misdeeds. This is the only way you can both accept responsibility for and thus, learn from them. Both are essential in developing sound judgment.

You will meet people in life, who are rich in intelligence and judgment. Acquire from both, for each has knowledge to offer. But if I had to choose whose lessons were more valuable and enduring, I would choose the instructor of judgment. You can learn trigonometry today and forget it tomorrow, without any need for it. You will always have a need for judgment.

Consider a **lesson** to be a commodity of knowledge and in that a commodity demands capital to be acquired, so too does a lesson. I have often told you that there are two types of lessons in life, the soft and the hard. Capital for the soft lesson is listening. Capital for the hard lesson is pain. You usually have a choice of what lesson you elect to pay for. You can purchase with your listening or purchase with your pain.

Understand the difference between "hearing" and "listening". **Hearing** is the ability to detect and process sound. **Listening** is the ability to distinguish and interpret what you hear. Learn to listen because you must listen to learn. And listen to all types of people, even the fool, for she/he can teach you how not to be foolish.

One of my greatest teachers was my mother, your grandmother, Joan. Her death on April 29, 1999, just a month before your birthday, was a great loss to me. Unfortunately, you will never directly receive the benefit of her counsel.

When she passed, I decided to put all I had written to you into this book. Much of it either came from her or was enabled by the foundation she laid for me. I only hope this effort serves as both a grateful and suitable tribute to her, as well as a torchlight for you, in her absence.

Thankfully, I learned to listen to Joan early on in life. By the time I was eight, she had given me the two greatest lessons I have ever received. The first of these came when I was five.

A family pet died and it was the first time I experienced the death of someone or something I knew. A few weeks later, my parents lost a friend and decided that taking my brothers and I to the funeral would be an ideal time, to teach us about dealing with death.

At that age, I did not process much of the event. But I did remember the environment and the people. We were in a church. Everyone was quiet. Some people were holding hands, others rubbing one another's backs. Some were hugging and many were crying. Later, at the repast and as the evening went on, the heavy emotions gave way to lighter moods. Many people were smiling, laughing and enjoying the food.

Two months later I was the ring bearer at a wedding. While at the alter, I felt nervous and looked around for Joan's reassuring smile. I also noticed that people were acting much the same way those had acted at the funeral. And later at the reception, just like at the repast, people were smiling, laughing and enjoying the food. Now I knew the two events were totally different, so I found all of this to be confusing.

While sitting alone at a table, staring out of a window, Joan approached me. She had been looking for me, to be included in some photographs. She noticed that something was bothering me and asked what was wrong.

I responded perhaps as only a five-year old could, "Why do people cry?"

At that moment, my mother knew exactly what I was getting at. She made the connection and recognized the confusion I was in, from observing the same patterns of behavior at the funeral and at the wedding.

She instructed me to look out of the window at the grass, the flowers, the birds and the squirrels. She explained how they all needed water to keep growing and to stay alive. Without water, everything living would die. Then she told me something I will never forget, something I want you to always remember:

> **"Inside of you and everybody is something called a 'soul'. It keeps you alive. Every now and then, you have to water your soul to stay alive. Tears are water for the soul. So never be afraid or ashamed or confused about crying. We all have to do it, to stay alive and to keep growing."**

Since your absence from my life, I have been doing a lot of growing.

I received my second most important lesson one summer day, in 1968. I was riding with my mother in her car, a huge powder blue, convertible Buick Electra 225, otherwise known as "a deuce-and-a-quarter".

While driving down what was then South Park Avenue, later named Dr. Martin Luther King, Jr. Drive, my favorite song came on the radio. I immediately started dancing in the front seat.

Then without explanation, Joan reached over and turned off the radio. I shot a look at her, part confusion and part anger. She had a mocking smile on her face.

I asked her why she turned off the radio and she said she would only turn it back on, if I gave her the definition of a word. This was a game she often played with me and one I never liked, particularly at that moment.

She said, "Tell me what 'think' means?" I figured this was easy. I go to school. I think all the time. I'll tell her and finish listening to my song. But to my frustration, I could not come up with a definition. Still today, I challenge many adults I know to do so and they cannot.

As my anger grew, so did Joan's amusement, which I thought was cruel. I knew exactly how much of the song I had missed and that it had yet come to my favorite part. As my anxiety boiled to a fever, she asked, "What are you doing to give me the definition?"

I yelled at the top of my voice, "I'm thinking!" Then I ducked. But that's when she really started to laugh.

Then she asked, "What are you doing to think?"

I paused for a few seconds and thought about that. For a seven-almost-eight-year old kid, this was a profound moment. What was I doing to think? I started to answer, "I'm asking…" and she interrupted — "That's it."

"That's what?", I asked.

"That's it. **To think means to ask a question**. If you're not asking questions, you're not thinking. Always ask questions." And with that, she turned the radio back on.

Always ask questions. Always, always, always. Your failure to do so means you will become a slave to ruling perceptions, rather than liberated by discovered truth.

These two lessons have enabled me to learn everything I know in life. Hopefully, you will find them equally fruitful.

Identity

When you were nearly four, I realized that you would be going to preschool soon. It would be the first time you would regularly be amongst a diverse group of children of different races and from different economic backgrounds. I wanted to teach you that those differences weren't significant, that what people looked like meant far less than what they acted like. I wanted to teach you that what mattered most was a person's inside, his/her character and personality. So I got an idea.

As Easter neared, I drained an egg and dyed it with many colors. I placed that egg next to a plain, uncooked egg. I took you into the kitchen and asked you which one you thought was the better egg, which one you wanted most. You picked the dyed egg. Then I instructed you to open it. As you cracked it, you were surprised and disappointed to find that it was empty. Then I cracked the plain egg. As I poured the white and the yolk into a bowl, I explained to you that this egg was more valuable. With it, I could make you something to eat. With the dyed egg, I could make you nothing. All you had was a cracked shell.

Then I explained that people are a lot like eggs. To find their real value, you have to get a look at their insides, because their outsides could just be pretty shells holding nothing. I encouraged you to make friends, as if you had to choose between the two eggs.

Then, with the plain egg, I made you French toast for the first time. You liked it very much.

I believe there are four cornerstones upon which life's foundation is based: identity, intent, family and spirituality. If they are all present, solid in their construction and designed with integrity, almost anyone's life can be assured of fulfillment.

Identity is the most important piece of the foundation. It can advance intent, overcome family dysfunction and enable a more purposeful cultivation of spirituality.

I reason that identity exist in two forms, based either upon physical reality or conceptual application. The first, **physical reality identity**, is the most commonly adopted, promoted and sought after. Why? Because we are visual creatures and derive our first information and judgments, whether accurately deduced, triggered by insecurity or programmed from bias, from what we see. Hence, our tendency is to both "display" our identities and judge the identities of others from their "displays".

This means physical reality identity is contingent upon an ability to define the material state of your appearance or existence, or the consequence of being defined by it.

On the first point, we live in a society obsessed with the perceived value of brand names and labels. If you have one type of logo on your shirt, you're one kind of person, another logo, another kind of person. Drive a certain car, you're one kind of person, another car, another kind of person and so on.

This brand-name fixation is not limited to mass-produced, commercial products, for we extend brand-name values and discretionary premiums to our neighborhoods, educational institutions, churches, synagogues, mosques and most particularly, race. Not only do we judge the Harvard grad more able, the Park Avenue resident more successful, the Holy Name Cathedral parishioner more committed and European Americans more esteemed, but we also judge them more worthy, more fulfilled, more morally true and more American.

Subscribing to this formation of identity creates identity devaluation, for the person with a $10,000 reality is judged less significant than the person with a $100,000 reality, who is judged less significant than the person with a $1,000,000 reality and so on. Whether observing the consumerism of America or the caste system of Hindu society, this outcome is true.

There are many harmful and adverse effects to this, but three I want you to consider most. A physical reality identity can:

1. Eviscerate your self-esteem.

2. Lead you towards a problem-plagued existence of longing for and constructing a superficial identity, beyond your means to attain and maintain.

3. Create a narrow focus of who you are, which will inhibit your character development, render you judgmental and reduce your valuation of yourself and others.

On the second point, the consequence of being defined by your physical reality, a more entrapping effect results.

The most valued physical reality identity in a society is that of the dominant group. Given that they disproportionately influence society's focus, their identity is disproportionately promoted and viewed.

For example, in a male dominated society, male identity reigns. Men are portrayed more in positions of power, control and influence. The word "man", a biological gender-specific distinction, still prevails as a general reference to everyone, even though women are the primary sexual species.

Likewise, in a racially diverse society, whatever racial group in charge is promoted more often and more favorably. A scan of magazines, television programs and movies bears out that "all-American" is considered European American. So when women ask of men and Blacks ask of Whites, "Why can't you treat me like a human being?", the answer is "what is a human being" is defined as "what is male" in the first example, and "what is White" in the second.

Historically, these physical reality identities and others have been sanctioned and supported by force. But a more sophistic promotion has proven considerably more serviceable.

Mythology. On one hand, it can serve as a mental security blanket, providing us comfort during the darkness of our emotions. Many a children's story and much of folklore can attest to this. But it also offers an opportunity for identity construction, when our imagined self falls short of whom we really are. As historian James Horton states, "Mythology tells us something we want to believe about ourselves." Extending that reasoning, it also tells us what we want to believe about others. To that end, mythology becomes an agent for constructing perceptions. Use it to convince, compel or control thought and subordinate behavior can be engineered.

Consequently, mythologies are constructed and assigned to the dominant group and all subordinates, to support and advance physical reality identities. History is slanted, revised, falsified and deleted, legends are manufactured and stereotypes are created and promoted as truths.

Accordingly, as the mythology of the dominant group institutes their superiority, the mythology of the subordinates decrees their inferiority. Here lies the trap I wish you to avoid. If you are not of the dominant group and consider the prime component of your identity to be an aspect of your physical self, you will become codependent to an inferior assignment. More than likely, you will either:

1. Fall prey to incorporating stereotypes into your core identity.

2. Squander a lifetime of energy in defiance or appeasement of them.

On the first point, this is why many African Americans insidiously use "nigger", the most vile of racial slurs, as a term of endearment. A well used maxim states, "You are what you think you are." The truth in this is that self-characterization defines one's constitution, the fiber of the being. In that African and European Americans alike see skin color as a significant, defining distinction, the consequence of promoting and incorporating disparaging stereotypes has mutually become a critical and noxious component of our identities.

On the second point, this is why famed tennis star and humanitarian Arthur Ashe once stated, that his greatest regret in life was all the time he had to waste being "Black". To accomplish his goals, he was forced to expend enormous energy to overcome perceptions and judgments created by the mythology imposed upon his skin. He felt that energy could have served a greater good, both personally and socially. I am sure that Jackie Robinson would have agreed, as perhaps would Billie Jean King, with respect to gender. And the outcome of a mentality directed by appeasement is crystallized in this quote, by entertainer Bill Cosby:

> "I don't know the key to success, but the key
> to failure is trying to please everybody."

Contrarily, if you are of the dominant group and consider your physical distinction to be the prime component of your identity, you are susceptible to developing:

1. A social myopia that will inhibit, even prevent your acceptance of those not like you.

2. An alliance to a tribalism that will make you both a prisoner to the paranoia of lost status and an accomplice to the violation of others either by direct action, inhumane indifference or the silent consent of cowardice.

I feel a more constructive identity to be one based upon a concept of who you are, for concepts transcend what is physical. Such an identity will allow you to exceed your visible limitations, as well as those people seek to impose upon you. This is because **conceptual identity** answers the question, "How do you value yourself without interpreting your physical composition and without regard to any valuation given by others?"

Your self-esteem will be exponentially enhanced, when advanced by a metaphysical projection rather than a material assessment. For example, the greatest concept known to the human mind is "God": a being who knows all, has created everything, is everywhere, has the power to start and stop on all levels and the ability to determine the fate of anyone or anything. This is a being to be feared, revered, worshipped and obeyed.

Throughout history, men have assigned this concept to their physical reality. The masculine promotion of "God" is clearly evident in the world's three dominant, monolateral faiths: Judaism, Christianity and Islam. In them, "God" is referred to as "The Father", "He", "Him", "His", "King of Kings", "Son of Man".

This conceptual assignment should not be underestimated. I have heard many a so-called feminist say "Our Father..." and subsidize patriarchy in many ways with their contradicting behavior. More than physical coercion, convincing women that the greatest thing they could ever interpret will always be a man is quite enslaving. And once White males applied this concept to their physical reality, via the Caucasian representation of religious figures, most notably Jesus, their domination was a foregone conclusion, despite representing a fractional minority of the world's population.

I would never suggest you assume an arrogance that declares yourself a god. Arrogance, like vanity, jealousy and denial is a foot soldier for insecurity. And insecurity is the greatest threat to the stability of an identity, for it wages war on self-esteem and self-expectation.

What I am suggesting is that your identity's foundation be your ideological self, rather than your physical self. Be what you think, rather than what you are. It is far more empowering. This is why Stephen Hawkings, a man whose body is ravaged by amyotrophic lateral sclerosis (Lou Gehrig's disease), can be regarded as the most brilliant physicist since Albert Einstein. He is his mind, not his body. This is also why slaves continuously risked death for freedom. The bondage of their bodies was not the bondage of their minds. Though enslaved, they never thought of themselves as slaves.

Do not go through life with an identity based upon a definition of what it means to be a gender, a race, an age, a resident of a neighborhood or what you can purchase. Those are all bricks in the pyramid of what it means "to be human". To define yourself or to allow yourself to be defined by one brick means to reduce the total value of your being.

"To be human" is the entire pyramid, the total sum and substance of a person, not one aspect of her/his form. And since "to be" requires mental direction, "to be human" is defined more by thought and the behavior it produces and less by physical composition. Again, what you think is "who" you are.

When I began my explanation of identity, I stated that it is the most important piece of life's foundation. That significance has yet been addressed. As I clarify it now, please take it to heart. I want you to understand this more than anything I have written. I believe it to be the most important instruction I can impart to you.

The word "destiny" means an ultimate fate. It comes from the Latin "*destinare*", which means "to determine". All that you do in life will help determine the arrival point of your fate. That point is your "destination" or how close you end up to a destiny. For example, human arrival into another galaxy might be the ultimate fate or destiny of aeronautical engineering. However, so far the moon has been its accomplished destination.

Many are the vehicles for travel to a destination — a bike, a car, a train, a boat, a plane. Some are more effective at arrival than others. The better your vehicle, the more likely your destination will be your desired destiny.

The vehicle for your life is your identity.

Read that line again and again until it becomes a mantra for your conduct. Destiny, to the degree that you can determine it, is contingent upon how you define, interpret and project yourself and your abilities. This is why the son of a billionaire can end up a drug addict in a gutter, or the daughter of a fourth-generation welfare, single-parent mother can end up the CEO of a major corporation. Your beginning doesn't always determine your end, because you are born into a situation, not an identity.

You must define that. So construct your identity carefully, maintain it with diligence and base it upon a value intrinsic to yourself, not a value contingent upon someone else or some group.

This will enable you to give priority to your emotions, opinions, decisions and intuition — the "north", "south", "east" and "west" on the compass dial of your destiny's journey. As a result, you will be less vulnerable to being directed by insecurity or the manipulative, sometimes abusive bearing of others. And once more, establish your identity to determine your total humanity, not one component. You cannot maximize your effort for a destiny, while minimizing your notion of who you are.

When I was thirteen, I saw a television program that questioned what animal really was the "King of Beast". It changed my life. The documentary began by capturing the prowess of the lion, the majestic king of predators. Later on, there was a scene of a pride resting under the shade of a tree. In the background, about fifty yards away, an adult male elephant emerged from some tall grass and bushes. The elephant was interested in feeding from the tree the lions were under. As he approached, he began trumpeting to alert the lions to move. Some got up, others were reluctant. Then, as if insulted by their refusal to leave, the elephant began charging towards the tree. Having closed the range to about ten yards, the remaining lions got up and fled.

The guide commented that if the lion is king and he will run from an elephant, then the elephant must be his emperor. As the film progressed, there was a scene at a watering pond. Other animals, zebras, wildebeest and the like had come there to drink. However, when the lions arrived, those animals scattered away. Next, a lone adult male rhinoceros arrived. As he approached the pond, with complete indifference to the other animals present, the lions immediately retreated to a distance away and waited for the rhino to leave before resuming their drink.

Behind the rhino, approaching the pond from lower ground, three adult male elephants appeared upon a small hill above the water. They stopped in their tracks when they saw the rhino. He never lifted his head. After he finished and left, the elephants proceeded to the pond.

Someone in the safari asked the guide why the three elephants did not scare off the rhino, as the lone elephant had done to the pride before. The guide responded by saying that the rhino is not a predator, so he has no intention to harm other animals. However, the elephants know that the rhino is the only animal, aside from another elephant, which could kill them and none of them wanted to risk a confrontation. He then suggested that if the lion was king and the elephant was emperor, then the rhino was the supreme sovereign amongst beast, the most powerful potentate.

Soon afterwards, to prove this to the safari observers, the guide pulled out a rifle and began firing at the top of the rhino's back. The bullets were skimming off of him like tossed rocks bouncing across an ocean. The guide then explained that the rhino was as close to an armor-plated animal as there was. And though not as attractive as the lion or not as large as the elephant, he was magnificently impressive and virtually invincible.

He also stated that rhinos are very near-sighted, with a clear viewing field of only 5-6 meters. He added, philosophically, that the rhino did not need great eyesight for he felt no fear. Therefore, he only focused on his destiny with little concern for the intentions of other animals. And as long as they didn't impede his destiny, they had no threat of being gored.

That day, I "became" a rhino. Though I could not physically metamorphisize into another animal, I adopted two rhino attributes as components to my identity:

1. I will live my life with the vision of my destiny and will not be deterred or distracted by the motivations of others.

2. The insults and disparagements people choose to fire at me will bounce from my spiritual armor, as the bullets had done off the rhino's back. They will not penetrate and injure me.

Now you know why I have often told you, that the rhino is my favorite animal. This is what I mean by conceptual identity. I tried to plant a seed of understanding about this within you, when you were six years old. It was then, I wrote this poem for you to learn:

I AM

I am more than what you see.
I am the strength of the mountain.
I am the energy of the ocean.
I am the glow of fire.
I am the freedom of air.
I am everything, all the time.

At that early age, I wanted you to begin to think of yourself beyond your physical reality. Since all things in the world come from an environment based upon these four elements — earth, water, fire and wind, I wanted you to see yourself in everything you saw. I felt that someday, if you could understand this from the poem, you would be able to construct, maintain and establish your conceptual self. Again, be what you think because there is no limit to thought. I hope you come to understand this.

On a final note, recall what I suggested when explaining enlightenment: you are not likely to meet many people in life with impressive and distinctive individuality. It is far easier to be assigned or to assume an identity, than it is to unearth or establish one.

Do not fear discovering or celebrating your individuality. Many are conditioned to such a fear, for social indoctrination often equates individuality with anarchy. This is why from birth we are directed and instructed to be in certain clans, to interpret group identity as what determines the individual. This is also why we tend to look at the marketed images of others, for what should define us. Consequently, most people go through life reducing individuality to a superficial exhibition of looking different, rather than discovering individuality as a personal resource.

If you ever get a chance to hear the song, "Let Me Fall", from the Cirque du Soleil *QUIDAM* performance, do so. Buy it and listen to it whenever you need to be reminded, that discovering your individuality is worth whatever effort you can apply or risk you dare to take. I have heard nothing in my life that better expresses this, than that song.

Intent

When I was fourteen, my mother's first cousin, Jimmy Rivers, gave me one of the most meaningful bits of advice I have ever received. I remember the day, March 15, 1975.

He told me to take a "Crazy 15", an instruction that meant at the end of each day, I had to sit down and write for fifteen minutes about anything. He reasoned that to find your life's purpose, you needed to keep a clear head. When you write, you learn to use what you need and to throw out the garbage that fouls up your mind. As he put it, "You gotta write out the crazy in your head."

I've been writing ever since.

Life is energy and that energy must manifest itself in some way, be it the wiggling of a baby, the work of a surgeon, the deception of a con man or the engagement of war between nations.

As you can deduce from the examples above, life's energy can have a constructive or destructive outcome. What directs either is purpose, an intended effect or a desired goal. Comprehending this, you can answer the question of the ages: What is the meaning of life? And in the answer you will realize that life's purpose is not the same as its meaning. Confused? I'll explain.

Physiologically speaking, life's purpose is to survive and reproduce, to make it to the next generation. This singular objective is an intended effect and a desired goal evidenced by all life, everywhere, regardless of intelligence. Even bacteria demonstrate this aim. On the other hand, life's meaning is a metaphysical construct derived from whatever purpose you assign to your living. This is a subjective, personal determination whose aim can be as varied, as there are people on earth.

A scene from the move City Slickers conveys this with profound simplicity. At one point, Curly (Jack Palance) offers insight to Mitch (Billy Crystal), in an effort to ease his sense of aimlessness. Curly advises that the secret to life is in finding one aspiration to pursue with passion, and by so doing one will come to understand what life means to them.

I realized my first, clearly defined purpose in life, by age eighteen. In the aftermath of my parents' divorce, my mother devoted her life to her children. My father occasionally devoted his time. His inability and lack of earnest conviction for parenting had a depreciating effect on me, almost equal to the benefit of my mother's dedication. The resulting disappointment and deprivation I felt provoked a strong motivation within me. Despite my youth, I decided that what I wanted to be most was the father to a child, my father never was to me.

Your "living" purpose is correlative to your identity. A positive identity will direct constructive development. A negative identity will direct destructive engagement. However, whether your identity is positive or negative, your energy will default to destruction absent a living purpose. Recall the example of fire I gave earlier. Guide the flame and it can yield many benefits. Left unchecked and fire will destroy completely and indiscriminately, to its own end. Such is living without purpose.

Your living purpose is your **intent**, an aspiration defined and fashioned by your own desires and expectations. If identity is the vehicle for destiny, intent is the direction of its course. The sooner you determine one, the sooner you are on your way towards your destiny, not your destruction.

Pursuing your intent will enable you to experience **passion**, the intense emotional energy of unwavering motivation. Without this energy, the gap between what you want to happen and what you make happen will always be great. While at college, I met a student from India who shared with me an Asian proverb that emphasizes this:

> "To attempt to manifest what you want without
> passion is like dressing up a corpse."

Furthermore, to live without this feeling is to live without full animation, for passion christens your zeal and yields the greatest of reward and disappointment, elation and dismay, joy and sorrow. Either way, to feel greatly is a pinnacle achievement in life, for no tear taste sweeter than that cried for the rapture that is passion's windfall.

Relative to enlightenment, nothing will present a more promising opportunity for self-knowledge than to define your purpose, and execute the effort required to seek it to its actuality. That effort can be likened to what is necessary to transform a dull, ordinary clump of carbon into an exceptional diamond. As I said before, concern yourself with the labor and you will discover your brilliance.

An adage holds that there are two types of people in the world: those who think they can and those who think they cannot — they are both right. Therefore, living with intent means having the mind and will to actively pursue your aspiration.

The key words here are "actively pursue", for it is much easier to state an ambition, a conviction or a purpose, than it is to live it. This distinguishes the dreamer from the doer and hypocrisy from integrity. And it is critical for your aspiration to be of your formation and not of someone else's. Your resolve must be free from the opinions of others, in order for your destiny to be true to your spirit, for no one can feel your desire as you do.

Also, understand that intent conveys self-expectation, which is a product of self-value, which is effected by identity. Again, I cannot impress upon you enough how critical it is to develop an identity based upon your intrinsic value, and with the expanded motivation to define your total humanity.

Two months before you were born, I decided to write down my intentions as a father. I did so because I wanted to clearly establish my parental purpose and to have it available for reference, to scrutinize and reinforce my efforts. My "Statement of Intent", written March 6, 1989, reads as follows:

As a father to any child I am fortunate enough to have, I intend:

1. *To teach my child a "healthy love"; a love that protects, preserves and promotes self; a love that does not make him/her easy prey for the harmful intentions and disregard of others; a love that will not intentionally harm or disregard others; a love that will construct, nourish and shelter not destroy, starve and reject; a love that will contribute, replenish and recycle not exploit, diminish and discard.*

2. *To help my child develop a conceptual identity, rather than one based upon her/his physical reality. A physical reality identity is limiting, leaving one subject to the contrivance of visual interpretation. This is what enables almost every form of discrimination, in the human realm. An identity that is limiting will produce a limited mind. A mind that thinks with limits will govern a life of limitations. Conceptual identity is based upon an ideological premise and is therefore limitless, for the boundaries of the human mind no doubt mirror the boundaries of the universe. For my child to have this type of identity, means he/she will travel beyond the horizon most people confine themselves to. It means she/he will actualize and not just realize life.*

3. *To always discover and never prejudge my child's potential, for a child is a flower in bloom, a flower no one has seen before. So who can know its beauty before it opens? Who can make a tulip a rose or an orchid a lily? No one. A parent is both the soil and the gardener. I can help germinate. I can water. I can fertilize. I can prune. I can weed. And then I can watch my child grow. I never want my frame of reference to cripple his/her ability to reach. I only offer it as a preliminary foundation for her/him to expand upon. Hopefully, my*

soil will prove fertile and my gardening will help cultivate maximum growth.

4. *To teach my child the distinction between religion/theology and spirituality and that the latter is more preferable, in that it is an extension towards others rather than an exclusion of them. Spirituality values the human, not just the convert, for spirituality recognizes the interconnected dependency of all destinies, rather than promote a tribal differentiation that asserts one destiny to be more important, more deserving and more entitled than another.*

If I can never employ my intentions with you, know them as I have so disclosed and engage them on your own, if you find them to have merit.

There are many downsides to living without intent. I consider the three worst to be:

1. The arrested development of or inability for introspection.
2. A life dominated by insecurity.
3. Hopelessness.

You can be sightless to the world and still attain your destiny. However, to be sightless to yourself is akin to standing blindfolded near a cliff, not knowing which direction to proceed. Take a step and you may walk off the edge to your peril. Become paralyzed with the fear of uncertain direction and you will go nowhere. Go nowhere and your anxiety may turn into bitterness for being unable to advance. And by chance should you walk towards a safe plateau, you will still find yourself without the vision to determine your fate.

Introspection is inner vision. From the Latin "*intro*" + "*specere*", it literally means, "to look into the inside". It is the ability to examine and evaluate your own thoughts, emotions, sensations, conduct and capabilities. The importance of this bears directly upon enlightenment and destiny. In order to know who you are, you must audit who you have been. And "who you are" is your escort to the future.

Beyond the shallow marketing of nostalgia, the contrivance of political "spin" and what is fashionably "retro", our country finds little value in introspection. Consequently, you are not likely to meet many people who possess a great capacity for it. This is most regrettable, for introspection gives sight to the "mind's eye". It allows you to see the morality of your conscience, the merit of your deeds, the truth of your motivations and the essence of your soul. And its vision is magnified by intent, for no constructive purpose can be achieved without self-examination.

The outcome of an inability to see inward is a constant looking outward. A fixed external focus will render you blind to your state of mind, because it disallows the process and summation of personal review — **reflection**. Without reflection, you will be unable to fully interpret, digest and express satisfaction, appreciation, gratitude and generosity — **the knowledge of valuation**. And without this knowledge you will be unable to experience **fulfillment**, the highest measure of satisfaction, appreciation, gratitude and generosity.

A life without fulfillment is an aimless pursuit to satisfy the hunger for meaning. Hence, a fixed external focus will subject you to a tortuous condition of mental, emotional, psychological and spiritual starvation. This condition can lead you towards a life of physical indulgence, because the unsettling urge of hunger creates a restless anticipation to be content.

However, a Catch-22 reality exist for an indulgence provoked by the hunger for meaning: the more you gorge, the more profound your emptiness will become, for its depth and perimeter will grow with every attempt to stuff it. Fulfillment is spiritual, not physical.

Over time, the vacuum of that emptiness will intensify and develop the draw of a black hole. A black hole neither radiates nor returns light. To "radiate" and "return" means to give out and to give back. Therefore, the consequence of this emptiness is that it will impair your capacity to give. This defines **spiritual gravity**.

Understand that from giving comes the **light of life**, an energy of active existence which has both, physical and metaphysical connotations. It verifies reality, for our first experience of light occurs at the moment of birth. Conception, gestation, labor and delivery all comprise the "giving" that creates that moment. This energy is also the exuberant motivation and jubilant vitality beaming from children and adults who appreciate the greatness of life. Their emanation is a gift of optimism to us all.

Each time the **act of giving** is done a "birth" is effected, like the giving of instruction for the birth of knowledge; the giving of compassion for the birth of solace; the giving of inspiration for the birth of hope. Perhaps no better summation of this exist, than in the confirming words of one of history's greatest statesmen, Winston Churchill:

"We make a living by what we get. We make a life by what we give."

The light of life is renewed and intensified by each act of giving. It is the torch within that can illuminate the path of your internal exploration, for the magnitude of your giving is affected by your awareness of what you have to offer.

Accepting this, I appeal for you to consider that a good deed is a seed of kindness that must be planted, in order to taste the fruit of gratitude. Both gratitude and generosity are essential for the knowledge of valuation. Therefore, your inability to offer consideration, goodwill and assistance to others will deny you fulfillment.

The significance of giving is lost to the draw of spiritual gravity. Its absorption constitutes the worst type of selfishness, one by default rather than conscious desire. The difference here is that conscious desire allows for recognition of motive and if a problem can be recognized, it has a chance of being remedied. However, the selfishness of spiritual gravity has no register on the radar screen of self-awareness, because without introspection self-awareness cannot exist. A person so disposed is defined by an <u>incapacity</u>, not an unwillingness to give.

Surrender to spiritual gravity and you will promote its selfishness. You will neither radiate nor return the light of life, and will be tinged by a darkness that can be visible in your physical appearance. Don't let this happen to you.

Steer away from those you see it in. Their recognition of and compassion towards the needs of others is critically skewed by self-absorption. No amount of effort, on your part, to put light into them will ever be returned to you. To the extent that they give out or give back is merely the lure of their neediness, which can magnetize your compassion and bring you within range of their pulling force. Over time, they will consume your enthusiasm for life.

Such people are directed by fugitive emotion, for interaction with them is contingent upon their evaluation of your usefulness. Their primary regard for people and things is determined by the ability to diminish their hunger, immediately and continuously. This is the essence of cynicism, for as an Oscar Wilde maxim asserts: a cynic is a person who knows the cost of everything and the value of nothing.

When you detect that people desire you mainly for the function you provide for them, judge them not to be your friend. Once your function has been exhausted, they will discard you. Lose them before they use you. However, if you choose to or find it necessary to engage with people like this, do so only to the extent that your benefit from them is equal to or greater than their gain from you.

This function-directed behavior can be evidenced in people who confuse "pleasure" for "happiness". **Pleasure** is an experience of sensation, a state of being. It is a measure of sensory gratification, brought about by an external source. And the duration of that gratification is fleeting, because it is based upon the physical presence of the source. To see a wonderful smile might be pleasing. When it stops, so too does the visual gratification it brings. To smell a rose might be pleasing, take it away and so goes the aromatic gratification it imparts. To taste a treat might be pleasing. When there is nothing left to eat, so ends the gastronomical gratification it offers.

Happiness is a judgment of meaning, a state of mind. It is an appraisal of spiritual disposition, which results from an internal recognition and celebration of fulfillment. Given that the span of that recognition and celebration can be quite enduring, so too can its happiness, for it is not contingent upon the physical presence of anything. If you live with the knowledge of valuation, just waking up is reason to be happy.

This is why many people can obtain the gratification of pleasure and still not achieve the fulfillment of happiness. With all concern directed outward and no knowledge of valuation, they cannot distinguish between the sensation of pleasure and the meaning of happiness. Their state of being becomes their state of mind, because the end result of spiritual gravity is a fixation upon your physical condition. A corporeal preoccupation determines the superficial value of everything and everyone with self-serving insistence.

Conversely, others can exhibit a level of fulfillment that seems unsubstantiated by their physical means. Their appetite for sensory gratification is not a consuming hunger, because their mind's eye allows them to recognize their spiritual satisfaction. They are content because of the abiding value they assign to their memory of the smile, the rose and the treat. Their state of mind becomes their state of being, for revelation is the end result of introspection. Revelation discloses the intrinsic value of everything and everyone, without the opportunistic demand of self-interest.

The ability to assess intrinsic value leads to the knowledge of valuation and vice versa. This reciprocal reality must first be consummated within you, in order to acquire introspection.

Similarly, a reciprocal reality exists between lacking introspection and developing insecurity. Without inner vision, you cannot see what calms your soul and insecurity is the ultimate spiritual agitator.

To feel insecure is to feel the absence of certainty, safety and stability. Everyone has insecurities, those worries in life that produce this feeling. However, for some insecurity is more than an emotional annoyance. It is a tornado of the mind: a foreboding, harassing, erratic and destructive neurosis that storms upon every aspect of their being. It directs their focus, filters their perception, brands their identity, determines their demeanor and fashions their personality.

There are obvious behavioral manifestations of people besieged by insecurity. I will offer an assessment of them, because I want you to be aware of these displays in yourself and others. Please do not consider and dismiss my assessment as a judgmental critique, issued by the alleged competence of an armchair psychologist. I submit it is an earnest dissection, explained with the caution gained from intimate knowledge. I have been one of these people.

My life has been dominated by insecurity, for most of its span. I know its whirlwind well. I have lost sleep from its thunderous presence in my brain. I have erred from its reckless contortion of my conduct. I have gasped from its suffocation of my spirit. So place stock in what I am saying. I speak with real-life experience.

In 1597, the English philosopher Sir Francis Bacon stated, "Knowledge is power." However more than 1900 years earlier, the Greek historian Herodotus trumped Bacon's assessment: "This is the bitterest pain amongst men, to have much knowledge but no power."

In order to fully comprehend the contrast between their opinions, you need to have a working definition of "power". A documentary called The Fire This Time, about the post-Rodney King verdict riots supplied one. I am not certain of who said it, but I have yet to find a more lucid, absolute and serviceable explanation:

"**Power** is the ability to define reality and to have
others respond to that definition, as if it were their own."

Though this definition was presented as a social-political construct, it has a personal utility. Quite simply, the ability to define a reality exist in varying degrees for nearly everyone, whether it be a painter's ability to define the reality of a blank canvas or a student's ability to define the reality of her/his scholarship. Insecurity cripples this ability, as it leaves you feeling unable to create, determine or effect the situations and consequences of your life. This defines "**powerless**".

Feeling this way is a precursor for emotional instability, because the infrastructure of your temperament is qualified by your perception to execute your will. The more able you feel to determine your reality, the more you will convey stability. The less able you feel, the more you will exhibit fragility. No one needs to look further than this truth, to understand the breakdown of social order following the Rodney King verdict. When enough weight is brought to bear upon a frail disposition, it will collapse. Such is the weight of that "bitterest" of pain.

Feeling powerless activates a constant sensation of being dominated, disregarded, imposed upon and imperiled regardless of whether anyone, anything or any situation has actually provoked agitation. This creates a preoccupation with victimization.

A person so focused lives life as if it were a midnight walk through the worst part of town, always on high alert for personal jeopardy. He/she has a self-perception as the potential or actual victim of malice and misfortune, while perceiving life situations and other people with the suspicion of mishap and violation. Forged from this perception is what author/professor Shelby Steele refers to as, "victim-focused identity."

This is the worst identity possible. To interpret yourself as a victim is to instate an existence of self-loathing and contempt for others, that makes victim perception a self-fulfilled prophecy. You will:

1. Corrupt your impetus for self-determination.
2. Sabotage the efforts of your aspiration.
3. Ignore the guidance of your intuition.
4. Divorce yourself from the responsibility of your behavior.
5. Hold everyone, but yourself, liable for every adversity that besets you.
6. Develop an entitlement mentality that seeks to leverage a victim status for gain.

Consequently, you will live a dispirited life of lowered expectation, underachievement and tremendous discontent. You will judge destiny to be something to wish for rather than obtain, in which case, you will reason your only remedy to either be a fortuitous grant of fate or the deliverance of a messianic emissary. Luck is a fickle suitor and messiahs are exceedingly rare. More than likely, your destiny will be a disaster of your making. And should you experience success, its fulfillment risks being bargained down by your self-devaluation.

I have observed six personality types spawned by insecurity and have lived as most of them. But before explaining them, you need to thoroughly understand the primal stimulus of all animals, that which is fundamental and universal to every living creature, especially humans.

The most compelling motivation in life is survival. Accepting this, two emotions above all others dominate every society — **aggression** and **fear**. They are the "essential" emotions, for they influence behavior upon the ultimate decisions of life and death. This is why our response to threat is characterized as "fight or flight". Correspondingly, every animal on earth can be separated into two groups: predator or prey. One must aggress to stay alive, the other must fear. Lions attack when they see zebras. Zebras flee when they see lions.

Insecurity modulates our survival emotions. It is the volume knob of our aggressions and fears. At a moderate level, we can interpret our motivations and anxieties with sane consideration. Turn that knob up to its maximum and clarity loses out to distortion. Turn it to its minimum and consideration is prevented by imperceptibility.

Such is the case with insecurity. Its distortion makes the otherwise coherent, incoherent; the soothing, agitating; the pleasing, insufferable. And its prevention impairs judgment, creating the hazards of unreliable deliberation.

Constant distortion will induce a highly reactive, uneasy state of mind, as a heightened concern for survival is accompanied by anxious arousal. This is why people defined by insecurity are often made uncomfortable by calm. Like everyone else, they need to validate and reinforce the determinants of their persona. If those determinants are fear and aggression that is precisely what will be sought. Tranquility supports neither and is thus considered foreboding. So they await the arrival of an unrealized disaster, react to the fantasy of threat and attack without considering the consequence.

People so directed have an emotional engagement with match-like potential: the moment contact is made, ignition occurs with no possibility to halt the flame before it appears. Likewise, upon registering emotion, they react instantaneously, employing little or no time to evaluate their feelings or reason the outcome of their behavior. Strike, flame. Feel, act.

This creates an incredible impediment for maturity, which is partly measured by the ability to reason out of an emotional state. When babies feel and act without rational filtering they are not disparaged, because they lack the maturation of judgment that comes with aging and development. However, when adults do so they discredit their character as being puerile and irrational. If your reasoning is compromised by emotional distortion, your lifelong predicament will be a clash between juvenile discretion and adult expectation.

You will see this in those with feel-act inclination. Their behavior can be impulsive, erratic and volatile. Their emotional progression often resembles a ride on an express elevator, going immediately to the top or the bottom, skipping all the optional floors of understanding, judgment and response in between. Preference is either love or hate. Feedback is either silence or rage. Desire is either dispassionate or fierce.

This is why they will often exhibit contradicting behaviors and make conflicting statements, in close proximity to one another. As their emotions vacillate, they will yield differing responses with jarring contrast. This can make involvement with them a confusing, irritating and tiresome task.

This may also help explain the puzzling grant of significance often displayed by those burdened by insecurity, for distortion and prevention tend to maximize in opposing fashion. What should be accommodated with slight significance is often given an exaggerated importance, beyond normal and reasonable rationale. And what should be given great significance is often reduced or discounted to no concern.

The personality types of insecurity exhibit these difficulties. Consistent with our survival emotions, they reveal either a fearful or an aggressive inclination, for feeling powerless induces a cowering or confrontational temperament.

Often singularly defining of a specific individual, the six types I have reasoned can be multiple traits displayed by one person, found in different combinations, surfacing at different times. The latter is true because of the emotional fluctuations and polarity insecurity gives rise to. It is also true because of the conjoined nature of fear and aggression. They are the Siamese twins of concern, co-establishing the persona of insecurity, as well as co-directing its behavior.

Over the years, I have named them. The first three describe people displaying "fear" personality. Their shared characteristic is a mentality of diminished value:

1. **The moles** are the most timid and prideless of the personalities, always yielding to their perceived importance of others. This is conveyed by their physical and social cowering. They are confidence gimps so discouraged by a fear of failure, they rarely demonstrate any desire or motivation to excel. Equally rare are acts of self-assertion, for they shrink from being contested or evaluated. Disputes and judgments are met with dreadful avoidance. They would rather accept blame, suffer imposition and take abuse than wager confrontation to defend or affirm themselves. With little capacity for adaptation, they find change unsettling and are addicted to routine. Terrified of risk, they are reluctant to spontaneity and adventure. Absent a sense of significance, they often register surprise, confusion or discomfort when given favored attention. Petrified of rejection, they feel unworthy and are made nervous by emotional or physical intimacy. Romance is resigned to fantasy. Consequently, they withdraw and become loners. They are the reclusive students who sit in the back of the classroom; the socially inept employees who eat a solitary lunch; the shy roommates who scurry off to the bedroom, when guest come by. The walls of their dejection are so dense, the energy of their frustration cannot escape. Hence, they are likely to implode when pressured. They are fatalistic and tend to view life as something to be endured. Their only solace comes from burrowing into obscurity.

2. **The panhandlers** suffer a persecuting hunger to be valued, in any way. Their dismal self-approval renders them spiritually indigent and unable to provide their own affirmation. So like starving

beggars who have not eaten in days, they are driven to desperation for the nourishment of being desired. Their destitution directs them pleading for whatever worth anyone is willing to assign them, no matter how slight, insincere or momentary. And as famine will drive one to scavenge from a garbage can to feast on the trash of others, their self-devaluation compels them to interpret any attention as good attention. They will seek it from the most debris-laden of people and are willing to endure almost any indignity to obtain it. Their loyalty and affection is wavering, as they are drawn to whomever will toss them a morsel of regard. Their helplessness to end their impoverishment and the humiliation it generates further eviscerates their esteem, which in turn intensifies their need for reassurance and praise. Most people who engage them, do so with transient intention and selfish motivation. Those who sustain involvement are either of like mind, in which case the relationship becomes a battle over competing needs; or they are driven by domination, in which case they tender a regard conflicted between desire and contempt. For these reasons, panhandlers become the pass-around-girls, the groupies, the battered wives, the yes-men, the bootlickers, the hen-pecked husbands. Their life is an unforgiving craving, made worse by a dependency on others to be fed.

3. **The pretenders** seek to endear value by campaigning for acknowledgment. They peddle a bag full of accommodations, bartering their conduct in exchange for affection and appreciation. Often gregarious and complimenting, they demonstrate an ability and willingness to communicate with anyone. Noted for charity, they give the unexpected gifts, surprise by doing the thankless chore, listen beyond the capacity of their tolerance. They are well liked and appear confident, assured and worthy of emulation. But they live with the wariness of being discovered as frauds. Their affability and charm is a disguise for a frailty that can be unveiled by one refusal, one disregard, one insult. Once exposed, they retreat like wounded animals away from the herd. Though sincere, their flattery and generosity equate more with attempts to remedy their feeble esteem, by enhancing the value of others. In romance, they choose Cinderella projects, hoping to effect self-admiration by transforming their mates. If their campaigning fails to produce fondness and recognition, they respond with a series of contrivances. They exaggerate emotions to draw attention; amplify anxieties to create concern; engineer suspicions to win over trust; fabricate legends to add to their dimension; manufacture dilemmas

to become a savior. They will even plunge into jeopardy, to set up their rescue. They are adept at creating dramas to star in. But their campaigning betrays them as they squander their talents to be well thought of, rather than using them for truly rewarding achievement and fulfillment.

The remaining three describe people displaying "aggression" personality. Their shared characteristic is a need to validate their value by displaying, constructing or engaging power:

1. **The headliners** need to feel and exhibit an importance validated by the recognition of others. With a longing to be glorified, idolized and venerated, they tirelessly seek status, often with mercenary morality. It matters not how they get it, just that they get it. And if unable to create their own, they will siphon it from someone or something of prominence, for they are cunning manipulators. Their value is proclaimed with the counterfeit confidence of arrogance and they expect everyone to subsidize their self-appraisal. Those who don't are dealt a condescending dismissal. A pompous pageantry of materialism markets their prestige. They believe everyone is envious, jealous and desiring of them. They hijack conversations to redirect focus to themselves and quickly abandon discussions they are not prominently featured in. They choose friends and mates based upon whether people add to the gloss of their veneer. They are the name-droppers and the trend followers; the actors always courting the camera; the crusaders championing any cause worthy of news coverage; the professionals always insisting upon being addressed by title; the athletes who often refer to themselves in the third person; the women yearning to be "Mrs. Anybody". Their tremendous investment in image renders them hypersensitive to judgments, criticisms and insults, as they rebut them with fire-breathing disdain. Often superficial, they tend to demonstrate depth only when relative to what distinguishes them. Though they often evolve in profile, they seldom do in spiritual development.

2. **The directors** find uncertainty unbearable and are consequently obsessed with control. They want to administrate everything and everyone, to insure their desired outcome. They have a dictatorial bearing and seek to intimidate, for they would rather be feared than loved. Those challenging them are either tersely expelled or ruthlessly targeted for retribution. They are very political, always

plotting, scheming and pressuring others to advance their objectives and expand their influence. They are intensely guarded and fiercely defensive. They have a palpable aversion to rules, regulations and authority figures, for they interpret themselves as ultimate sovereigns. They are predacious and target involvement with people who quickly yield to challenge or are emotionally vulnerable. Their friends are viewed as agents of their volition, rather than goodwill companions. They have a proprietary regard for their mates and are prone to irrational jealousy. People who have long term relationships with them tend to be dependent on or feel coerced by them. They are the overbearing mothers insisting compliance; the tyrannical bosses who often threaten and seldom thank; the selfish boyfriends demanding isolation from others; the pimps who prey on young runaways; the cult leaders instructing with a "god complex"; the husbands who beat their wives. In the end, they either become crazed when faced with the loss of control, the recipient of revenge from someone they violated or resign to a bitter loneliness, brought on by the alienation of nearly everyone they know.

3. **The "CJ's"** or **conflict junkies** are the most mercurial and malignant of the personalities and warrant the most explanation. They embody the complications of every type mentioned, raising them by the exponential component of self-contempt. They are troubled by a sense of worthlessness so vexing it becomes its own entity, a virulent antagonist always harassing and bullying their peace of mind. It is the demon within, assaulting their self-esteem with brutal hostility. Their only solution for valuation is to attack it. However, their conflict is self-addressed and directs hostility inward. This means their attack equates with self-aggression, which compounds the conflict for it runs contrary to feelings of self-preservation. So they displace their hostility, turning it outward. To overpower the demon, they must overpower others.

   Nothing demonstrates power like confrontation and destruction. One offers the chance to prove might is right and the other confirms absolute domination. It is the need to demonstrate that distinguishes this personality type. CJs are always instigating confrontation or creating destruction. These acts are their drugs of choice and they need them to lay the demon to rest. Given this, they are both dealer and fiend, supplying the narcotic of power for their addiction to conflict.

They possess what political commentator Eric Sevareid once referred to as the worst type of power, "the power of shamelessness". This is the ability to act without any moral or ethical deterrence. People so disposed are malicious opportunists and are capable of taking sinister beyond the grasp of human comprehension. Conflict junkies are so capable. They harm, vandalize and demolish rashly, randomly and routinely. If they feel they have been wronged, they will respond with the severity of a nuclear assault. They will brand themselves the ultimate victim and retaliate with the intent to annihilate, even if destroying you means destroying themselves and all around them. This makes them the most dangerous of all people, for they act with no register of loss. They will attack both reputation and body. Not only do they lie, they believe their untruths. Not only do they kill, they believe they are justified. They are spiritual terrorists incapable of feeling remorse or taking responsibility for the transgressions and atrocities they commit. They never apologize.

At times they will appear submissive. This is just a ploy, as they adjust to a disadvantaged or new situation. The ominous hint in their eyes always betrays them, so learn to recognize the ruse. Since their focus is always directed outward, they are the most impaired for introspection. This makes them acutely critical of others, what they cannot see in themselves. And since they are driven to diminish, they cannibalize the value of their mates. Involvement with them often results in violation.

Like the other personality types described, but even more so for CJs, everything is personal and personalized. Hence, their self-contempt is highly combustible and detonated by the slightest pressure. Conversations with them can be likened to a walk through a minefield. You never know what might trigger an explosion, so avoid them at all cost. They are the women whose scorn Hell's fury is no match for; the thugs who perpetrate senseless acts of violence; the stalkers who murder when rejected; the suicide terrorists who find virtue in their forays; the hate group leaders who urge the ruination of all not like them. Their destiny, almost always — self-destruction.

Study these descriptions well to safeguard against their development in you, and to make possible your sensible interaction with those who represent them. Again, your greatest protection against insecurity is an identity that validates your intrinsic value, and an intent that relies on that value to execute a destiny. Value and intent bring about the certainty of conviction, and certainty is the antithesis of insecurity.

Also, invest in **truth**, that which is obviously undeniable, rationally irrefutable and demonstrably clear. It will adjust the distortions of insecurity and counter the misgivings, machinations and mendacity it sanctions. Truth is insecurity's kryptonite.

Now, the final consequence of living without intent. A life without actively engaging a constructive purpose is reactive, not proactive. It means realizing a condition, not actualizing an ambition. To live in such a way gives rise to **spiritual oppression**, the feeling that life is a forced burden and that there is no way to effect change or alter its course and outcome.

To live in this state creates a toxic brew of emotions: resentment, anger, fear, dejection, helplessness and abandonment. These emotions are very acidic and gradually erode will. They disintegrate the optics of inner vision, causing blindness to those resources necessary to survive, overcome, create, thrive and succeed. And they corrode resolve, breaking down all motivation and commitment for the pursuit of any destiny.

This leads to the utterly overwhelming and thoroughly convincing belief that the condition will only worsen and never end. And this will effect <u>the single greatest threat</u> to sanity and life, **hopelessness** — the state of spiritual collapse.

It is hopelessness that makes some people disillusioned to possibility, unresponsive to opportunity and apathetic to change. They become the "candle gazers", sitting idle and abject, watching and waiting for their flame to go out.

It pushes others into lifeless resignation, unwilling and unable to apply any energy for hope's ignition. They are the zombies, the spiritless robots barely capable of executing the rudimentary functions of life.

Some become totally disconnected from rational existence, their mental cohesion dissolved away by the toxicity of despair. Theirs is a solitary confinement to melancholy. Unreachable, they are forever lost to bleak isolation.

Finally and most lamentably, it is hopelessness that so debilitates and weakens others, they are no longer able to hold on to their lifeline. So they lose grip and free fall towards the ultimate act of surrender, suicide.

Neither the entitlement of race, the advantage of gender, the immunity of status nor the application of wealth can vaccinate against hopelessness. Intent is the only prevention and the only cure, as it:

1. Provides direction to keep your identity on the road to its destiny.

2. Offers and replenishes the fuel for your journey, the energy of motivation.
3. Reveals your inner treasures, allowing recognition of your intrinsic value.
4. Makes you an active participant, rather than a passive bystander to life.
5. Enables inner vision, which is necessary for you to continuously see the future.
6. Produces the knowledge of valuation, without which you will not experience fulfillment or know true happiness.
7. Gives your life meaning, which yields a force that can repel the pull of spiritual gravity.
8. Makes the light of life inextinguishable, so that you will always see your capacity to give.
9. Shields you from the perils of insecurity.
10. Keeps hope alive.

Family

The most I ever felt "family" was on a surprise trip. When I was nine or ten, my father was given a vacation to Las Vegas, as a bonus from his company. He and my mother decided to make it a family affair. So they secretly arranged for my brothers and I to be dismissed from school for a week.

When we went to the airport to see them off, my grandmother and uncle came along. As a treat, my parents allowed us to board the airplane, since we had never been on one. As we listened to the flight attendant speak, my brothers and I realized it was time to get off, but my mother and father insisted we wait because there was more time before the plane departed. In less than a minute, we were being told to buckle up and the plane's engines began to roar and vibrate. My brothers and I were alarmed and that's when my mother told us we were coming along. It was great. There we were, excited, happy and together. Nothing was wrong.

Everything was right.

Family is the atom of society. This is a statement often said, never disputed and perhaps never more in need of understanding than now. Destroy that atom and the "matter" that is society ceases to exist. Many a slave trader and despot have realized this truth. One of the keys to Hitler's rapid expansion was to separate families from themselves, upon invasion. Once achieved, the immediate disintegration of that town, city or country would ensue.

Unfortunately, your family has been splintered since your were two. This is very regrettable, because it means one of the cornerstones to your foundation has already been compromised. Consequently, the remaining three are at risk for instability.

However, this does not mean you are resigned to a crumbling life of discontent. You can repair, reinforce even rebuild your base, making it stronger than its initial construction. To do so, you must first have a clear idea of what defines a family and what it should mean on a personal level. I will offer my opinion for your consideration, but I urge you to purposefully examine and contemplate a definition and meaning, on your own accord. Whether it does or does not reflect what I suggest is not the point. What matters is that you can never have, what you cannot first define. If you want family, you must determine what "family" is.

I believe family is not defined by biology or surnames. Relatives are. This is why people who have worked together for many years, soldiers in army barracks and even members of a sports team can consider themselves family. Because what defines "family" is a feeling and one feeling, more than all others, is the critical determinant. Trust. No relationship, whether instructional, professional, familial, romantic or with self can be constructive and developmental without a foundation of trust. I attribute such importance to this emotion, because of how I define it:

Trust is a condition of confidence that
your vulnerabilities will not be exploited.

Those who seek to exploit your vulnerabilities are parasitic opportunists, only concerned about their welfare. They are unworthy of trust. Your involvement with them will only lead to your devaluation, demise or destruction. Likewise, for you to exploit the vulnerabilities of others for your selfish regard and to their detriment, makes you an agent of this opportunism and equally unworthy of trust.

Without this condition of confidence, no other emotion — love, devotion or caring can exist in truth. Because anyone who would ignore you in need, or value you only to the extent that they can use you or take advantage of your weakness does not truthfully love you, is not truthfully devoted to you and does not truthfully care about you. Think about it, you will not speak to someone you do not trust, but you can choose not to speak to someone and still love them. It is the relationship emotion, upon which all others are contingent.

Therefore, **family** is a relationship of great unity, forged from and held by the bond of trust, which enables all other nurturing emotions to flourish and enrich those joined by that bond. Consider that bond to be the umbilical chord of belonging, which makes family the psychic placenta for the individual.

Never feel obligated to honor, endorse or subsidize a family bond, even with me, if you cannot feel trust and especially if you have evidence of distrust. The term "family" is not an exclusive license for those you are linked to in blood or in law. Instead, it is a covenant to be mutually entered into, by those you feel trust with. It can be broken by abuse, neglect, deceit and betrayal. Accepting this, you can reason the possibility of repairing, reinforcing and rebuilding your base, for your "family" can be constructed and assembled from the people you know now and will meet later.

After your mother and I divorced, I had great concern about the register of trust between us. I feared you would view my departure as deserting you and that you would blame me for the upheaval that followed. I also feared the real potential for disruption of our relationship and thought it essential to bolster our bond, at every opportunity. So on many occasions when we were together, I would take you to a park for an exercise in trust.

I would blindfold myself and allow you to walk me around, by holding my hand. You were only three years old then. I had to trust that you would keep me from the hazards of bumping into poles and people or from stepping on uneven ground and tripping. You always enjoyed this game and eagerly looked forward to playing it.

After several weeks, I began switching roles and would then lead you. Every time out, we were each able to stay blindfolded for a longer period, until we finally felt no discomfort in being led by one another. Without ever mentioning the word, I knew I had convinced you to trust me.

Perhaps this is why, despite all the time that has separated us, on those rare occasions we have seen one another you have still given me affectionate reception. I am encouraged by those displays and remain optimistic that our trust bond has not been severed. Regardless of how tenuous its current existence may be, that it could exist at all holds the promise of reconnection. A threadbare present can be rewoven into a solid future. Someday, I hope to walk with you again.

As you consider the significance of family, you should evaluate the meaning of the relationship that initiates most families. Marriage. Romantic idealism describes the popular view of a quest for a lifelong union. Marriage is regarded as the ultimate physical and emotional relationship, a virtuous pursuit of monogamous devotion inspired by transcending love.

The facade of that idealism has long been exposed, something you must realize with your own parents. The dismal rate of divorce, abandonment and unwed pregnancies prevalent in our culture provides even more evidence. There are perhaps as many causes for these consequences, as there are people who experience them.

However, I have long suspected that one of the greatest obstacles to matrimonial bliss lies with the origins of marriage, as a legally sanctioned and culturally recognized union. Since most people are unfamiliar with the historical derivation of statutory wedlock, they are destined to perpetuate its original intent. Someday you might choose a lifetime mate. I would hope that the idealism many dream of becomes a realism you enjoy. So I want you to have an awareness of the initial motivations that ordained marriage as a social contract, to enable your evolvement beyond them.

As an institution endorsed and authorized by theological doctrine and secular law, marriage did not originate from love's direction, but rather from the politics of sex:

1. So that men could determine the paternity of their children. Everyone knows the mother of the child. This is one major reason women have been more harshly judged for infidelity, because it creates doubt about fatherhood.

2. So that men could claim ownership of women. This reason ushered in the custom of women taking on the last name of men. The claim of ownership is adjunct to reason #1. A man's child must bear his name to declare his paternity, although matrilineal naming is more truthful, in that a woman is the only certain parent. Also, patrilineal naming gave men more assurance about passing on property and estates after death. Furthermore, ownership designation of women as chattel meant that they could also be used to satisfy debt. This was and still remains a practice and is partly responsible for the custom of "fathers giving away the bride". This economic element is also associated with the practice of polygamy. Not only was it a cultural convention to provide for widows and unmarried women of a community, but also one used to display a man's indulgence and wealth.

3. To insure the continuation of aristocracies and monarchies. Hence, marriages were arranged, often times before the children were even born. Arranged marriages also evolved as provisional insurance for women, given their historical denial of financial self-determination and their consequential economic dependence on men.

As you can see, the origins of legally sanctioned marriages had more to do with patriarchy than love. In fact, other marriage customs can be linked to this directive. The "best man" came about, largely out of a practice of abducting women for marriage. When maidens were not available, men would kidnap them from neighboring towns, villages and hamlets. This was a risky, often dangerous undertaking and required assistance. So the desiring man would ask his brother or best friend to accompany him for the task.

This practice of abduction is also a contributing element to the custom of women standing at the left of the alter and the best man, to the right. The family of the kidnapped woman would attempt a retrieval. With swords being the common weapon, it was necessary for the right side to be clear for combat, since most men were right-handed and drew their swords from their left sides. Therefore, women were placed to the left. The "best man" stood to the right as the first line of resistance, in case his friend had to escape with the kidnapped maiden. For this reason and the three mentioned earlier, I have never worn my wedding band on my left hand. I wear it on my right as a constant reminder that spouses are equal in importance.

I learned these things by reading books like <u>How Did It Begin</u>, by David McKay and <u>*The Christian Book of Why*</u>, by John C. McCollister. Make the effort to investigate the matter on your own. That way you will begin the necessary and personal process of determining what marriage should mean to you.

In my opinion, the chauvinistic orientation of matrimony has given it a functional character with as much, if not more cohesion coming from executing duties, as from feeling emotion. That orientation still exists, despite the idyllic notions people subscribe to matrimony. Who pays what bill, manages the children's activities, takes out the garbage, services the car and does the grocery shopping are issues that qualify the lives of most couples, not the passion and elation that drew them together.

This poses a great threat, for a primary valuation of utility reduces the humanity of a person to need, not elevate it by desire. The most extreme example of this is slavery. I would caution that if need dominates desire in a relationship, it is at risk for violation or termination. When reduction is a principle ingredient in the concrete of a marriage, as it sets, emotions will evaporate, indifference will infiltrate and contempt will eventually wear away the foundation.

Case in point. Industrial societies suffer more divorce than tribal/agricultural societies. In industrial societies, women have more opportunities for economic independence. And overall, people have a better chance at individual determination, rather than being dependent on the group reliance of tribal cultures and agricultural economies. Consequently, relationship cohesion is weakened, which threatens the longevity of marriage.

This predicament is not likely to diminish, while being supported by a porous foundation structured for need. The base of marriage, set upon the bedrock of trust, must be solid enough to allow for the continuous construction of desire.

The character of a marriage is not unlike the identity of an individual. Function is physical. Sound familiar? I have already pointed out the pitfalls of physical reality identity versus the advantages of conceptual identity. I contend that if more people had a conceptual theme for their marriages and not just a dreamy illusion, fewer relationships would degrade to functional execution and instead be upgraded by ever-increasing devotion.

A conceptual theme provides a matrimonial intent, to which a directed and concerted effort can be made. It is more than a spoken generality, for which people have no specific application in their lives. I offer my concept as an example.

The union of women and men can be viewed from an evolutionary perspective. Billions of years ago when life began, all reproduction was asexual, effected by fission or cloning. Asexual reproduction did not provide the genetic diversity evolution was dependent on. By replicating the same thing over and over again, there was little possibility for the adaptation necessary to adjust to changing environments or combat new pathogens.

Nature solved this problem by splitting the life form into two entities, female and male, dividing the genetic matter for total composition into two separate beings. This created sexual reproduction and is why the genders must unite to reproduce. They must be joined again to continue life. That splitting also created an infinite combination of genetic couplings and is responsible for the incredible evolution and diversity that decorates our world today.

"Female" and "male" are gender distinctions applicable to 99% of all living things, plants and animals. Thus, women and men represent the two halves of the whole that is human. That we can make reference to development of one's "feminine" or "masculine" side indicates, that on some level, most people have an awareness of this.

As humans, we have many beings: physical, mental, emotional, psychological and spiritual. They are all capable of extraordinary development. But the highest level of personal evolution occurs from the connection with others that brings totality.

That we can unite through intercourse to produce life, verifies both our dual distinction and dependency. Therefore, as gender entities we are not alien to one another, inhabitants from different planets who come together to produce confusion, as popular culture continues to suggest. We are complimenting, compatible, shared beings whose connection on a mental, emotional, psychological and spiritual level is as vital and as possible as our connection on a physical level. What was once one, became two. To become one again, that two must come together — on all levels. All of our beings must be reunited.

Conceptually speaking, this means **marriage** can be thought of as an attempt to reunify the separated human, or what I sometimes refer to as "asexual reunification". Just as I could not become the rhino physically but could philosophically, so to is the possibility of this concept. It means seeking a union with that one person you believe best completes your humanity, the importance of which I stressed earlier when discussing identity.

If that sounds selfish, it should. Selection of a friend is a selfish exercise, for it is based upon subjective desires and the perceived enhancement of one's life. Selection of a marriage mate must then constitute the most selfish exercise, in pursuit of friendship. It means selecting someone deemed more desirable than all others and judged best to enhance life. Furthermore, those efforts we are most committed to are efforts we selfishly regard. If we personalize the goal of marriage beyond desire for someone, we might be more inclined to demonstrate more devotion to it.

This concept does not mean that what distinguishes male and female persona has to be nullified, in order to succeed in marriage. Gender distinctions are essential to our continuation and those distinctions are reflected in the multiple beings we represent. What it does mean is that our aspiration for completion requires the symbiosis and synergy of "what is male" and "what is female" to be "what is human". For that completion to be accomplished, the dividing and often fabricated conflict of gender disparity must be afforded no accommodation.

Unfortunately, the religious and secular definitions and promotions of marriage, as a union based upon "being a man" and "being a woman", formalizes and institutionalizes gender disparity. Both establish and endorse a functional existence to marriage, by designating duties and assigning roles unique to the husband and similarly so, to the wife. Such duty designation and role assignment is neither valid as being gender specific, nor considerate of an effort to bring humanity into a marriage.

I believe from the concept I have proposed, matrimony can evolve and expand beyond the limitations that now threaten it. It does not have to be a fixed arrangement bounded by physical function and dependency. Instead, it can become a thriving intimacy representing a boundless consent for personal evolution.

I believe such a concept will produce the ultimate self, the ultimate union and the ultimate love, because the selfish desire for completion must become an altruistic effort to be realized. Anything done to insult or injure, neglect or negate your mate becomes your affliction. Likewise, anything done to praise or protect, aid or advance your mate becomes your benefit.

When I began my perspective on marriage, I referred to part of its idealism as a virtuous pursuit of monogamous devotion. It may be easier to negotiate peace in the Middle East than to pursue monogamy. Though women and men alike are culprits to infidelity, men clearly surpass women as repeat offenders. From the vantage point of social indoctrination, patriarchy has always been duplicitous in its judgment of male and female behavior. Also, an argument could be made on behalf of evolutionary inclination. Genetically speaking, men are hardwired for a more constant and easily provoked stimulus for sex.

The contrary realism to our idealism of monogamy is that it is not the natural sexual disposition of most animals, regardless of gender. Very few species exhibit it with any regularity. The dictates of survival have always motivated animals to seek as many opportunities as possible, to advance their genes to the next generation.

However, the elitism of humanity seduces us into thinking we are "other than" animals. But that is what we are, albeit more neurologically developed, but animals nonetheless. The same primordial DNA that began more than 3.5 billion years ago and has since been built upon to establish the entirety of the animal kingdom, can be found in the genetic matter of humans. Before its completion, the Human Genome Project has already brought to light that about 95% of our genetic composition has been passed on unaltered, since the Stone Age era which began some 750,000 years ago. We are likewise motivated for survival.

Does this excuse infidelity? No. To the extent that behavior is ordained by genetics exist a variable, perhaps as enormous as the population of the world. It is not solely compelled or orchestrated by biological direction. Were this to be true, hypnosis and brainwashing would be impossible and the notion of free will and the exercise of restraint would be nonexistent.

We are endowed with the capacity to make choices and with the ability to understand the consequences of our choices. That endowment is the gift of "intelligence" and the execution of "judgment". Our intelligence allows us to construct in the abstract, to propose an idealism or what we hold to be a desired perfection, a preferred excellence. Our judgment allows us to strive for it. Monogamy is one such idealism, what we hold to be a relationship perfection. Without an aim for perfection, relationship involvement regardless of type, would no doubt revert back to the base motivations of a dog-eat-dog society. Nothing is improved without an aim for perfection. Nothing.

In that monogamy is a concept and not a natural state, perhaps you will find it even more convincing to invest in a conceptual foundation for marriage. To do so makes monogamy far easier to achieve, for the effort becomes less one of overcoming a primal urge and more one of channeling your energy for you own perfection. That we can reason and dedicate ourselves to do so for a better body, a college degree or a higher salary and not marriage is not only ridiculous, but a cop-out on integrity. Is it difficult? Yes. Is it worthwhile? Definitely. The less you are diverting to others, the more you are investing in your mate and ultimately, yourself. So the issue of monogamy is more one of personal development and less one of genetic motivation or moral integrity.

Now about love, that emotion most focused upon in relationships. Of all things I have sought to define and understand in life, love remains the most confounding. Consider this: it is difficult to look at a circle and figure out the point that began its drawing, but to look at a circle, you know exactly what it is. Such is the case with love.

It is a feeling whose measure can be the volume of an eye dropper or the expanse of the Grand Canyon. Its effects can be as viperous as venom or as life giving as Mother's milk. Its memories can be as haunting as a nightmare or as unforgettable as a vision of paradise.

So what is love? Most people would define it as an intense feeling, desire or consideration, a definition equally serviceable for hate. So why are they perceived as opposites? Is it that one builds while the other destroys? One nurtures while the other starves? One elates while the other deflates? In my lifetime I have been bolstered by, experienced the agony of and have soared and crashed from feeling both love and hate. So what distinguishes them?

Inherent to love is affection, appreciation and a desire to develop. Inherent to hate is disdain, depreciation and a desire to destroy. So what "love" is depends largely upon the motivation of who is feeling the emotion. Perhaps this explains its many contradictions and confusions, because love is influenced by the magnetic pull between the poles of "what we feel" and "why we feel".

However, if I were to suggest a meaning for love, it would have to be one given by my sister-in-law, Mary:

Love is the ultimate measure of value.

Understanding this, you will realize that your deepest feeling of desire and preference, your highest expression of worth and gratitude and your greatest demonstration of care and dedication all apply.

I would caution against being seduced by the "notion of love". I can best explain this by recalling one of my favorite songs, as a teenager. The Spinners, and R&B group popular in the 1970s, recorded a song entitled "Love Don't Love Nobody". If you can pardon the double negative, you will realize a profound truth and reduce the risk of suffering the foolish heartache of falling in love with romance, rather than with people. Unfortunately, as the song also testifies to, it took me a long time to learn this.

Love is not a person, a being or an entity in and of itself. That is to say, "love" does not love, people do. And the words "I love you" are not Cupid's incantation to be recited as a magical chant, for a "happily ever after" relationship. However, many people behave as though feeling love and verbalizing it are all that is needed, to insure the success of a relationship. "Happily ever after" is the fictional ending of fairy tales. Relationships are real-life associations, connections and ties. People must realistically deal with their realities.

To say "I love you" is an expression of tremendous emotional investment. That investment must be genuinely regarded, responsibly considered and thoughtfully nurtured to yield the joy of its potential. Beyond this, I can offer no more clarity, except to say that love must be experienced to be known and a life without that experience is the most tragic of all circumstances. So what I will offer are five recommendations about how to experience it. First, recall "My Statement of Intent", regarding how I wanted to father you. The initial objective dealt with instructing you to have a "healthy love":

> "...a love that protects, preserves and promotes self; a love that does not make him/her easy prey for the harmful intentions and disregard of others; a love that will not intentionally harm or disregard others; a love that will construct, nourish and shelter not destroy, starve and reject; a love that will contribute, replenish and recycle not exploit, diminish and discard."

Without this type of love, you may develop a behavior that will sanction or subsidize denigration and exploitation, as standard components of a relationship. Your experiences will likely harm others or prove harmful to you.

Secondly, love is not an endless reservoir that you can draw from at your discretion. Just as the clouds above and the oceans below return water to one another, you must constantly restore emotion to your loved ones. Otherwise, your experience will be that of an emotional nomad on a barren desert always searching for the next drink, or it will leave you as depleted as a useless well.

Third, understand that the occurrence of "ünconditional love" is as rare as finding a four-leaf clover. Furthermore, believing that you should tender it can be as reckless as driving while intoxicated. If love was unconditional, dogs would never leave their owners, an alienation of affection between parents and their children would be impossible and divorces would never occur.

Even the God of Moses, Jesus and Ishmael preconditions His love with the Ten Commandments and will punish for noncompliance. To love without condition is to forsake your self-preserving value. Do this and you will all but guarantee an experience of violation. You must be able to assess the conduct in others that will cancel your love in them.

Where as the other recommendations apply to any type of interpersonal relationship, the fourth is more specific to romance. You will come to hear of "the working ratio" for a successful relationship, the 50%-50% equation of each mate making an equal effort to the union. I suggest that a 70%-30% ratio is better. Here is why.

A large portion of any relationship is defined by the care, contribution and compromise of those involved. But unless those involved are retaining some time apart, to engage and pursue the interests and activities unique to one another, they risk losing their individuality to the relationship. When this happens, the personal appeal that initially drew them together will dissipate, as will their desire for one another.

The 70% represents the care, contribution and compromise that should be equally regarded and demonstrated. The 30% represents the time apart, evenly divided for the purpose of maintaining the individuality of each person. No questions asked. Do this and your desire will not only endure, but intensify from an ever-increasing appreciation of one another, rather than chance being diminished by the resignation of role-playing.

The fifth and final recommendation requires greater commentary. It is about forgiveness, an issue nearly all relationships confront at some point.

Biblical text instructs us to "turn the other cheek". This defines "forgiveness" as an act of absolution that pardons the guilt of an offender by not retaliating, penalizing or punishing. To do so restores the stature, esteem and value of the offender to the status held before committing the offense. But there exists a great disparity between the ambition of religious doctrine and the reality of life.

Relative to religion, it is difficult to reconcile the instruction of "turn the other cheek" with the obvious contradictions of other biblical descriptions, accounts, codes and creeds. Both Old and New Testaments are full of punishments, penalties and retaliations, beginning with the rebuke of Adam and Eve; the story of Cain and Abel; the plagues of Moses; the Great Flood of Noah's Ark; the destruction of Sodom and Gomorrah; the apocalyptic tone of Revelations.

An argument could even be made that biblical text is a supreme advocate for capital punishment, for it is laced with God-edicts of death punishments, like the sentencing of death by stoning for the loss of virginity. If the God originated by Judaism, interpreted through Islam and esteemed by Christianity instructs us to turn the other cheek, to absolve and pardon the guilt of our offenders, why does He offer Heaven and Hell — eternal reward and eternal punishment? There is certainly nothing forgiving about living forever in damnation.

I think these contradictions illustrate the difficulty of trying to resolve the conflict between what we are and what we want to be. Remember the earlier quote by James Horton, "Mythology tells us something we want to believe about ourselves." Religion, as mythology, attempts to mitigate that conflict, but in so doing demonstrates that it too is strained by the difficulty.

True forgiveness is not a grant dictated by religious dogma. This is why most of us do not "turn the other cheek", despite declaring some sort of religious adherence. This is also why we are willing to accept the apparent contradictions of biblical instruction. To know the realism of transgression is to know that the idealism of "turn the other cheek" forgiveness, is an invitation to more transgression. This is quite clear when it comes to marriage. At the time of this writing, America's divorce rate exceeds 54%.

True **forgiveness** is a conditional redemption, which is why penance and atonement are advanced through religion, as spiritual remedies. Consequently, forgiveness is possible when the offender is perceived to have demonstrated sincere remorse for the transgression, and provides convincing evidence that his/her behavior has been transformed by an amended mentality.

To ask for forgiveness, without demonstrating remorse and providing evidence of transformation, is a self-serving request for an exemption from guilt and responsibility. To grant forgiveness, without witnessing remorse and seeing evidence of a transformation, only devalues redemption and excuses the offender without motivation to change.

The desire to retaliate, penalize or punish against violation is not only understandable, but essential to the establishment of relationships and the survival of civilization. Otherwise, why would we get divorced, dole out fines, build prisons, issue life sentences or speak of the "wrath of God"? Guilt should not be assigned to the feeling of being violated and recovering from violation does not necessitate the violator's redemption. Such thinking and instruction is partly responsible for the codependent mentality of battered spouses.

Additionally, denying forgiveness does not equate with substandard character, moral intransigence or an inability to advance beyond the emotions of a transgression. One can thrive in the aftermath of violation, for the victim's value is not contingent upon restoring value to the victimizer, the offender is not entitled to absolution for the offense and violation does not have to become an identity.

Understand this, so that you can both grant meaningful forgiveness and know what it means to seek it. Otherwise, your experiences with love are likely to be characterized by inconsideration, mistreatment and repetitious error.

Also, consider that you must be willing to forgive that which you seek forgiveness for. To not be so willing is moral hypocrisy. Double standards undermine the integrity of everything, even mercy.

Spirituality

When you were younger, you were afraid of the dark. I acknowledged that your fear was real and of great concern to me. So I made up a ritual to eliminate your bedtime fright.

I suggested that you were afraid, because you could not see what was in the room. Then I convinced you that what really frightened you, were the invisible spirits and demons in the air. I hinted that if you knew what demons feared, they would fear you.

So I "revealed" that what scared them most was not being able to breathe, because if they couldn't breathe, they would die. I then explained that since air burns, the single flame of a candle would burn off all the air for the demons to breathe. This would make them leave, to find air elsewhere. So at night when I tucked you in, I would light a candle and let it burn for five minutes, while I sang to you. You would stare at a digital clock, watching the five minutes pass, at which time you would peacefully fall asleep. You believed me and it worked. '

The light of your spirit can consume all that threatens you. But in case you forget, light a candle and remember that most of our fears are as weightless, as the air we breathe.

Never give air to the demons of your fears.

The final cornerstone of the foundation. It allows you to see your reflection in the face of someone you don't know. It enables you to listen to a song with no singing and hear every "word". It permits the communion you feel with Mother Earth, when alone in one of her many gardens. And it demands your awe when you stare into the sky and behold, that you are greater than the physical limits of your being.

What "spirituality" is has always been and still remains the subject of much debate. Regardless of perspective, that debate has generally been one of religious interpretation. Most people hold religion and spirituality to be so related, as to be interchangeable terms. So what I am about to say may shock and even anger you. That is a risk I am willing to take, if the net result is that you will question for a meaning on your own.

I do not regard religion and spirituality to be the same thing. Moreover, I consider them to be so dissimilar as to compare sand to water or grass to milk. I have met many people who are very religious and are spiritually clueless. Inversely, I have met people who are very spiritual and have no religious affiliation or adherence at all. To explain how this is possible, I must first address what I think spirituality is not, in contrast to religion.

The structure of religion is a belief in a deity (or deities), who in exchange for insuring circumstances of fate, demands the allegiance of a people and so decrees their tribal identity as defined against all others, not of similar allegiance. Whether that tribe is gender-based, ethnic, racial, cultural or nationalistic, this establishes a belief in separately ordained destinies, for each tribe sees its fate independent from and more deserving than others. Condemnation and conversion are reasoned to preserve the tribe's existence and future, as well as considered to be approved directives of the deity. Thus, the core objective of religion is the control of many, to insure the preservation and advancement of the tribe.

The effort to control many is more easily effected, by impressing the mind with an authority that responds to defiance with horrifying consequences. Recall my earlier explanation of the survival emotions, aggression and fear. Now understand that those who aggressively market fear, seek control. Though Niccolo Machiavelli analyzed and articulated this concept well in his book *The Prince*, he certainly cannot be credited for inventing it.

The aggressive marketing of fear has long been an instrument of great leverage, used by the architects of religion. Regardless of civilization or epoch, much of religion has been focused upon creating a culture of fear to establish control. To be taught that compliance or noncompliance of religious doctrine can determine one's ultimate and eternal fate is quite a compelling dictum. Neither the concept of Original Sin nor Hell were accidental inventions.

As a result, servitude, obedience and the repression of individuality feature prominently in most religions, with the threat of great penalty for lack of submission or conformity. It should be no surprise then that most people come to religion by indoctrination at birth, not by election from reasoned discovery in adulthood. Choice and control are often adversaries. The sooner choice can be restricted or eliminated, the sooner control can be established.

It should also be no surprise that the term "God-fearing" is used, to esteem an ideal religious disposition. Throughout my life, I have had many conversations with people regarding religion, spirituality and faith. The most significant revelation I have discerned is that no matter how devout or occasional their declaration of conviction, most people believe in a god because they are afraid not to. Their religious adherence is, in large part, motivated by a fear of harsh judgment from the community at large for non-belief, or by having a "get out of jail free" card to hedge against the uncertainty of an afterlife.

Very few religions succeed and proliferate, without constructing or benefiting from a culture of fear. However, a culture of fear sanctioned or utilized by religious dogma produces several undesirable outcomes. In my opinion, the two most consequential are moral hypocrisy and conflict.

On the first, all hypocrisy can be thought of as moral opportunism, be it born of moral duplicity, moral superficiality or moral flippancy. But to me, the most egregious hypocrisy is that born of an intentional manipulation of fear, given that the motivation to instigate and promote fear will reason and employ abuse to achieve its end. Abuse demands the respect of dread.

This truth has not been lost on the architects of religion, for once they have determined their moral ideology for the masses, they will abandon all moral subscription to enforce it. This indictment can be levied against most religions ever constructed, including Judaism, Christianity and Islam.

History and present-day situations provide abundant examples of this. There exist no shortage of religious leaders and followers willing to reconstitute or dismiss moral consideration, when an act that is morally consistent with their own doctrines contradicts their organizational motives or personal desires. Consequently, religious authorities and devotees will often excuse, justify and commit any act for the sake of forcing rule, coercing behavior and maintaining control.

Some of the most blasphemous acts ever committed in the realm of human experience have been executed on behalf of religion, and deemed worthy by whatever god whatever tribe esteems. The atrocities perpetrated by the imperialism of missionaries and The Spanish Inquisition are appalling citations. South Africa's system of apartheid was promoted as a covenant from God. Abortion clinics are bombed by people who consider themselves God's ambassadors, killing others to protest what they view as killing. Many acts of terror and brutality are committed by religious zealots around the world and promoted as God's justice.

The second outcome, conflict, has been more devastating. Religion accepts a notion of redemptive violence, particularly when purging the pagan, impugning the infidel and imposing moral authority. It was the 5th Century writer, scholar and theologian St. Augustine who formalized this notion with the Christian concept of a "just war". Today, every branch of the armed services has its version of a chaplain who blesses soldiers prior to combat, with the hope of a divine grant of victory.

The term "holy war" should be as outlandish as it is oxymoronic, in any language. However, history shows how perfectly compatible the words "holy" and "war" have been. The longest battle on record, The Hundred Years War (actually 116), was a religious crusade fought when popes were also commanders-in-chief of their own armies. For decades, Ireland has been ravaged by religious strife. Many other nations have reduced their populations, by investing in the murderous policy of "religious cleansing". And Jerusalem, revered city of convergence for Judaism, Christianity and Islam, is the epicenter for a region that could ignite the next and most costly World War.

Now regarding spirituality, I do not comprehend it to be the divine matter, composition or realm of any god or group of gods personified by human perspective. It is not contingent upon belief in, recognition of and devotion to a deity. It is not fashioned by allegory or structured mythology. It is not the exclusive commodity of one religion or another, offered as a reward for obedience or purchased by conformity and allegiance. It is not created or defined by rituals and written codes of conduct that are designed to control, convert or condemn.

Neither does spirituality institute tribalistic, divisive and elitist practices or identities. It does not demand unquestioning belief, from which an "understanding" is forged to live in accordance to a dogma. It invites questioning for understanding, in order to be convinced by what is fundamentally and undeniably true. Its truth cannot be manipulated to give power to some and to take it away from others. It is without a racial, ethnic, cultural, geographic or nationalistic designation or distinction. It is without a preferred gender or a defining sexuality.

I believe **spirituality** to be a universal essence sprung from the interaction of life. Like air, it is influenced and utilized by everyone and constantly surrounds us, whether we register its presence or not. Its reality is the interconnected destiny of all life. It can be positive or negative, exalted or evil. Its virtuous manifestation is a behavior directed by a focus upon unified destinies. Its vile manifestation is a behavior that rejects or is blind to that focus. The struggle and connection between the two is morality.

Thus, the essence that is spirituality is **the energy of behavior**. This energy, like light, is tangible and perpetual upon emission and active long after its source has expired. This is why we are still affected by and utilize the behaviors of Moses, Jesus, Mohammed, Buddha, Napoleon Bonaparte, Harriet Tubman, Abraham Lincoln, Susan B. Anthony, Albert Einstein, Adolph Hitler, Jesse Owens, Mahatma Gandhi, Joseph Stalin, Eleanor Roosevelt, Golda Meir, Mao Tse-tung, Dr. Martin Luther King, Jr., Richard Nixon, Mother Teresa. Their contributions to that essence are everlasting, as are the contributions of all who live, whether we are recognized by history or not.

An example of interconnected destiny would be deterioration of the ozone layer. As an industrial society, America has long produced pollutants damaging to the atmosphere of everyone on earth. Likewise, the Amazon Rain Forest, which produces 20%-25% of the world's oxygen supply, is under grave threat of deforestation. Both situations bode peril for humanity. Though we live thousands of miles from one another, our shared destiny is tied to our separate behaviors. If we lack or ignore awareness of this connection, our separate behaviors will spell our mutual doom. A spiritual focus would perceive this.

Another example comes from an African tale I was told, years ago. A tribe was experiencing great internal conflict and began splintering into different factions, all posturing to control the group. The leader of one faction was greatly troubled by this. Fearing bloodshed and the destruction of their unity, he reasoned someone must go into the jungle and seek counsel from the Wisest Man on Earth. He thought to choose someone young, to insure the advice would not be poisoned by a personal desire for power. So he selected a boy and stressed that the wise man's guidance was their only hope to restore harmony and save the tribe.

The boy, very frightened by being alone in the wilderness, pressed on knowing the importance of his task. Eventually he found the wise man and asked him for help. When he told of his problem, the wise man replied by asking, "Would you say that your tribe was living in Heaven or Hell?"

The boy responded, "Hell. Evil is present in their hearts and deeds."

The wise man then asked, "So what you have come to find out is what makes 'Heaven', heaven, and what makes 'Hell', hell?"

The boy thought for a moment and agreed, "Yes, that is the answer I need."

The wise man then told the boy to imagine a place where food and water were everywhere, ready to eat and drink and that there was no reason to hunger or thirst. But the people of this place were miserable, for they were all hungry and thirsty. Each of them had a spoon with a long handle fixed to one hand and a cup with a long handle fixed to the other. This made it difficult for them to feed themselves or to drink, for they could not reach their mouths with their utensils. So they walked about, taunted by the bounty and unable to partake of it.

Then the wise man said, "This is Hell."

Next, he told the boy to imagine the same place with the same people, spoons and cups, except this time everyone is happy. Then he paused to wait for the boy to respond.

Confused, the boy asked, "How can this be? If this is the same place, with the same people and the same spoons and cups, why are they now happy?"

The wise man answered, "Because they have learned to feed each other. This is Heaven. Go back and tell your people this."

Our behavior bears the awesome responsibility of affecting the lives of others, while we are alive and long after we have died. Perhaps if we embraced the linkage of our destinies and understood the continuum of our conduct, we would exercise greater care, compassion and concern for how we live our lives.

Without an awareness, understanding and appreciation of unified destinies, I fear humanity will never benefit from what I call "blood knowledge" — a complete recognition and reception for what is universally obvious and elemental to us all. Without this, we may never be able to derive a framework for morality, law and conduct that is applicable to all, regardless of language, culture, nationality, age, race or sex. Without that framework, we are destined to continue to actualize the worst of who we are. We will not prosper from the life-promoting, life-enhancing behavior and fellowship spirituality has to offer.

I want you to realize this, so that you might promote it through your living. But your realization can only come from an awareness of your value in others and their value in you; your dependence on them and their dependence on you; your link to them and their link to you.

If you accept my explanation, you will come to understand and cherish the paradox of being human: to be equally significant and insignificant, at the same time. From this you can know the "tangible intangible"— the substance, quality and dimension of your essence, your spirit, your **soul**. It is your soul that serves as both transmitter and receiver of the energy that is spirituality. Without cognition of your soul, you will either live as a spiritual mute or become spiritually dead.

To increase cognition you need to comprehend the difference between "being lonely" and "being alone". The first is a state of deprivation, the second is a state of composure. It is in this state of composure, when you can converse with your soul, the importance of which cannot be overemphasized.

You will never reach the summit of your humanity, the peak that completes your pyramid, without being comfortable in solitude. Ask anyone who has ever been to the top of "Mt. Everest", those people who have overcome great challenge and adversity, to scale a height of achievement and accomplishment most will never know.

If you can be quiet with yourself, you will hear the guide that will direct you to your summit. That guide, inherent in us all, is the pathfinder to spirituality. Listen to it. If you harmonize its guidance with the reality of unified destinies, you will elevate your individuality, your purpose and your sense of belonging to its highest height.

There are but three things I have left to share.

Perception

When I was in third grade, I read a story about a woman of modest means, whose best friend married a man of great wealth and social standing. Though her friend moved to a more affluent neighboring town, they remained in contact and continued to enjoy the warmth, kindness and affection their friendship had developed, since childhood.

One day the woman's husband received an invitation from his boss, to attend a stately ball. The couple interpreted it as a good sign that their fortunes would soon turn. The woman met with and told her friend of the event, who in turn offered use of some of her jewelry to make an impressive appearance. Initially hesitant, not wanting to risk damaging or losing expensive accessories beyond her means to afford, the woman eventually accepted the offer. Borrowing a majestic pair of earrings and a matching necklace, she assured her friend she would return them the day after the ball.

The night of the event was grand and her appearance was all the fantasy she had ever wanted. She was complimented frequently and her husband even thanked her, feeling his wife's impression on others would earn him greater recognition with his boss. Before the evening ended, his boss offered him a promotion with an interest in the business. Very happy with the news, the couple celebrated with great revelry. Soon, they thought, they would finally ascend to the social elite, as they had always dreamed.

The morning following the ball, they awoke to the dreadful reality that the jewelry was missing. Whether they had been stolen, had fallen off or been left behind in the powder room, the earrings and the necklace were gone. The couple was devastated.

What would she tell her friend? How would they replace the jewelry with their meager earnings? Those items cost more than what her husband earned in ten years. And he felt embarrassed, fearing that if the truth came out, he risked being ridiculed and losing his promotion. So they decided to tell no one and move out of town, reasoning that they would take on whatever jobs necessary and buy back the jewelry, to return to her friend.

It was twenty years of hardship, before they finally saved enough money to replace the jewelry. The woman became haggard, her beauty erased by the guilt, misery and drudgery that became her life. And her husband grew bitter and resentful, cursing her for ruining their opportunity for wealth and status.

After buying the exact pair of earrings and the same necklace, the woman finally revisited her friend to confess her misadventure. Upon entering the grounds of the estate, the woman saw her friend strolling and approached her. At first alarmed to see what she thought to be a beggar woman heading towards her, the friend was taken with compassion and embraced the woman, who had already begun to cry.

However, the woman interpreted the embrace as a sign of recognition and forgiveness and clutched her friend tightly, sobbing unmercifully in her arms. But it soon became obvious her friend did not recognize her and she was forced to reveal herself. Shocked and astonished by the woman's appearance, her friend began asking the woman about her condition.

That is when she told her story and presented the replaced jewelry, offering much regret and apology for what had happened. Her friend sat down, stunned. Then she explained to the woman that if she had revealed the truth twenty years ago, she could have told her that the jewelry was paste, not diamonds and worth no more than the shoes on her feet. She explained how it was customary for women of wealth to have replicas made of their jewels, so they did not have to risk being robbed or losing them. Her friend then refused to accept the jewelry, but the woman left, thoroughly ashamed, humiliated and broken. They never saw one another again.

Upon returning home to tell her husband what happened, she only found a note. He had left, blaming her for ruining his life.

That story so moved me, I never forgot it. I was struck by how perception can so dramatically alter both a life and how a person is interpreted, for **perception** is a subjective mental impression not an objective physical certainty.

From that story a seed was planted in me, later to germinate into one of the greatest realizations I have ever had: there is a tremendous difference between what is "fact" and what is truth. It was a "fact" the woman perceived the jewelry as being made of expensive diamonds. It was the truth the earrings and necklace were paste. It was a "fact" that her friend perceived the woman as an unknown beggar. It was the truth that the beggar woman was indeed her childhood companion.

Even our legal system recognizes this distinction, as it tests for "reasonable doubt" not indisputable truth. The objective of a legal battle is to construct a persuading impression, not qualify absolute certainty. Whoever succeeds in doing so, wins the verdict. If the real-life drama of the O.J. Simpson trial didn't bear this out, nothing ever will. Consequently, truth and justice are more the derivatives of subjective deliberation, than they are the by-products of neutral consideration. After all, perception is anything but impartial. Despite the judicial idealism that justice is blind, the personnel of a courtroom can and do see through the biased filters of their lives.

An attorney once told me, a **fact** is anything you can get three people to attest to in open court. Black's Law Dictionary defines it as, "a thing done;

an actual occurrence; that which has taken place." I state to you that Shaquille O'Neal is 5'3", weighs 120 pounds and is a circus contortionist. As a statement made, it has been done, has actually occurred and has taken place, as the words on this page verify. It is a fact that I stated it.

Black's Law Dictionary does not have a listing for "truth", so recall a definition I offered earlier when explaining insecurity:

> "...**truth**, that which is obviously undeniable, rationally irrefutable and demonstrably clear."

The truth is Shaquille O'Neal stands more than seven feet tall, weighs more than three hundred pounds and is currently regarded as the most dominant player in professional basketball. If you put him on a scale, measure his height and watch him play, this will become obviously undeniable, rationally irrefutable and demonstrably clear.

By fifteen, I began to realize that the world doesn't run on truth, but on competing perceptions — what can someone get you to believe. At that age, I started challenging commonly held perceptions, to see whether they were "facts" or truths. To demonstrate the critical significance of this distinction, I offer two examples for your consideration:

1. It is a "fact" that homosexuality has been theologically preached and culturally promoted as an abominable willful election, to be regarded as a moral dilemma of tremendous social and religious consequence. Sexuality is a core distinction. It exist more as a manifestation, not an intent. It is because it is physiologically effected, at least this is how heterosexuality is regarded. Yet willful election, not genetic causation, is the test of scrutiny for homosexuality, as willful election connotes volitional intent. However, it is a truth that homosexuality is found in a wide variety of insects and animals exhibiting sexual reproduction. No amount of theological or secular denial and condemnation can erase that truth. In that hermaphodism, an adjunct biological development that physically conjoins both genders in one sexual being, has a physiological substrate, why not the psychological or behavioral fusion of gender as sexuality? That the behavioral differentiation of gender as heterosexuality can be logically appraised for being physiologically ordained, and the behavioral concurrence of gender as homosexuality cannot is illogical.

   Homosexuality, like hermaphodism, should be regarded as evidence of the mutated evolution of an asexual organism into a sexual species. From one came two. Therefore, the variable for sex and sexuality is not two, for the gray area of shared genetic matter between females and males, men and women, yields progeny across a gradient of several possible combinations. A case in point, slime mold has thirteen different sexes. Imagine the politics of persecution that would provoke in the human realm. Even fruit flies, snails and grizzly bears exhibit homosexuality. And it can be reasoned with some degree of certainty, that they neither willfully elected it or are in a moral dilemma about it, nor we about fruit fly, snail and grizzly bear homosexuality.

The social reproach of homosexuality must be seen for what it is — a heterosexual anxiety whose discomfort has been interpreted as a justifiable contempt, via religion. But why would God be so selective in His disapproval? If He indeed created all creatures, why would He make present in many of them a behavior He judges morally objectionable only in humans? This apparent rational inconsistency and moral contradiction must be seen for the prejudicial contrivance it is. But it isn't the first time "God" has been used to denounce those others feel uncomfortable about. Nor will it be the last.

I recommend you read a book called Biological Exuberance, by Bruce Bagemihl. It is a great treatise on the subject of sexual diversity in the animal kingdom. I am convinced that after reading it, only those most resistant to reason, most seduced by sophistry and most prodded by prejudice can deny the obvious physiological foundation of homosexuality. Now, the second example:

2. It is a "fact" that Jesus Christ has been promoted to the world with a racial identity of Caucasian origin, portrayed with very Nordic and Aryan features: blond angora hair, blue eyes, keen nose, thin lips, pale skin. It is a truth that the Gospel of Matthew list Jesus' genealogy as being of Semitic and Hamitic ancestry, while the Gospel of Luke list His genealogy back to Adam, the first man.

   The words "*Semite*" and "*Semitic*" are biblically derived from Shem, one of Noah's three sons. Shem is biblically distinguished as the patriarch of the ancestral line to Abraham and consequently, King David. Davidic lineage is part of the prophecy of the Messiah, who Christianity recognizes as Jesus. Most Christian scholars agree that both Mary and Joseph were "of the house of David", as being of Davidic lineage.

Though the term "*Semite*" is used today in reference to Judaism and Jews, historically it is more properly a reference term for people of a region, as "*European*" refers to one from the region of Europe. Consult any dictionary and you will find the primary definition of "*Semite*" and "*Semitic*" to be "a member of a Semitic-speaking peoples of the Near East and Northern Africa, including the Arabs, Arameans, Babylonians, Carthaginians, Ethiopians, Hebrews and Phoenicians; of, relating to or constituting a subgroup of the Afro-Asiatic language group that includes Arabic, Hebrew, Amharic and Aramaic" (The American Heritage Dictionary, 3rd Edition).

In biblical times, people of this region were of many ethnic groups and faiths, not just Judaism. This is important to note given that the perception in America, by both Jews and non-Jews, is to regard "*being Jewish*" as a racial designation of Caucasoid distinction. It is not, for "*Jew*" and "*Jewish*" are religious-cultural designations, like "*Moslem*" and "*Islamic*" or "*Episcopal*" and "*Episcopalian*". Proof of this lies in the truth that I, an African American, can convert to Judaism and not change my race.

Furthermore, the term "*Jew*" is not solely a biblical reference to a member of the tribe of Judah, son of Jacob (also called, *Judahites*). It equally refers to one from Judea (also called *Judeans*), the regional name the Romans once assigned to what is present-day southern Israel and southwest Jordan. And many etymologists believe "*Hebrew*" was derived from the Egyptian word "*habiru*", which was used disparagingly as a general reference to all outsiders.

The word "*Hamitic*" is derived from Ham, one of Noah's two other sons, the third being Japeth. Ham is also biblically distinguished, though unfavorably so. He was cursed by both God and Noah (Genesis). His curse by God was for having sex while aboard the Ark, something God forbade. The punishment was "to be stained" and "smitten in the skin", in other words, to be made dark. Thus, *Hamitic* is a reference to being of dark skin. His curse by Noah was for seeing his father drunk and in the nude.

This curse, approved by God, was for all of Ham's descendants via his son Canaan, to be the "lowest of slaves…to his brothers". Thus, *Canaanites*, the progeny of Canaan, were a dark-skinned people cursed to be slaves. These biblical tales have been used throughout history, to justify both the enslavement of dark-skinned people and the condemnation of homosexuality as religious indictments, convictions and penalties. Such is the power of constructing mythology as divine authority.

Following the Great Flood, Noah's sons were sent out to repopulate the earth. Japeth is said to have been the founder of Greece and Shem, founder of the lands of Mesopotamia, now the Asian nations of Turkey, Syria and Iraq. Ham also established lands, as can be metaphorically inferred by the names of his sons Cush, Egypt, Put and Canaan. With the exception of Egypt, these nation names no longer exist. They encompassed portions of what is now Israel, Jordan, Somalia, Sudan, Eritrea and Ethiopia. This I learned by simply looking up these biblical terms in a dictionary and an encyclopedia. Moreover, Canaan is distinguished in the Old Testament as the "Promised Land" — the same land that later became Palestine and later still, Israel.

Descendants of Canaan became ancestors to the Davidic lineage via three women: Tamar, Rahab and Bathsheba. Tamar, mother of Perez, and Rahab, mother of Boaz, are identified as Canaanite women and of the ancestral lineage to Jesus. Bathsheba, who bore David's son, Solomon, is identified as a Hittite woman. Hittites were a Hamitic people, having been descendants of Heth, a son of Canaan. Moreover, the "*-sheba*" in "Bathsheba" actually refers to the ancient country of Sheba in southern Arabia, what is now known as Yemen. The people of Sheba colonized Ethiopia about 1,000 years before Christ. Again, go into any good library or bookstore and consult a reference like the Holman Bible Dictionary. This information is readily available.

Also, the etymology of the word "Ethiopia" is Greek and means, "of burnt land" and "Ethiopian" means "of burnt face". These terms were used by early Greeks to describe all people south of Egypt. This is significant, in that some theological scholars suggest Ethiopia to be Mary's ancestral homeland (research The Jesus Seminar). Nevertheless, these biblical genealogical references list a geographical and racial identity of Afro-Asiatic ancestry, for the descendants of Shem and Ham were people of color, Arabs and Africans. This coincides with references of Jesus, as having hair like "wool" and a body colored like "brass" and "amber" (Revelations, Ezekiel, Daniel). It is also supported by the truth that Jesus' spoken tongue was *Aramaic*, the Semitic language of the people of *Aram*, an ancient country referred to in the Old Testament, which is now modern-day Syria. Even as many continue to conveniently ignore the biblical references mentioned, most historians and theologians acknowledge Jesus' Middle Eastern-African ancestry, electing to describe His appearance as being "swarthy" — an adjective that describes and defines "dark skin", "brown", "dusky", "tawny", "sienna".

Furthermore, when considering Creationism and the birthplace of humanity, an equally notable "fact" can be assessed for truth. In Genesis, The Garden of Eden, that place Adam and Eve were "formed" and "ribbed" into existence by God, is geographically defined as a land that yields four rivers: 1. The Pison or Pishon, which passes through the entirety of Havilah, thought to be the land now defined by much of Arabia (Saudi Arabia, Yemen, Oman, The United Arab Emirates, Qatar, Kuwait); 2. The Hiddekel, the Hebrew word for the Tigris, a river that flows from Turkey through Iraq and into the Euphrates; 3. The Gihon, which is said to have gushed forth from the Kidron Valley, near Jerusalem and flowed through what was then Mesopotamia, later Assyria and now Turkey, Syria and Iraq and 4. The Euphrates, which flows through those same regions. The four rivers of Eden denote a vast area whose nations are consistent with the lands of Shem and Ham, especially when considering that Africa and Arabia were joined until the opening of the Suez Canal, in 1869. As a point of time-line comparison, the Civil War ended in 1865.

Whether considering Matthew's link through Shem and Ham or Luke's reference back to Adam, the promoted images of Jesus and other biblical figures suggest artifice, not accuracy. Check out the geography.

No less than Pope Julius II and the great Michelangelo can be charged as the greatest promoters of this racial fallacy, with the renderings of the Sistine Chapel. But as you can see, such popularly promoted imagery is not supported by the very Judeo-Christian theology it claims to depict.

Contrary to the historical revisionism of art, literature and film, "Adam" and "Eve", the first man and woman, were not milky white in complexion, something science has long recognized. Neither were the Egyptians a Caucasoid people, who spoke the King James Version of English with British accents. After all, The Exodus to the Promised Land was from Egypt to Canaan: from Africa in the south to the Mediterranean in the north. For that reason, Rameses II, Moses and the people he led from bondage did not look like Charlton Heston, Yule Brennet and Edward G. Robinson. Neither did Jesus, unless you are willing to suspend all rational plausibility to believe the great Norwegian navigator Leif Ericson looked a lot like me, just because I said so.

The "facts" I chose to examine are very provocative and controversial, to say the least. That is why I chose them, for their consequences have included the vilification, persecution, subjugation and death of millions of people. I want to impress upon you the caliber of distortions and misconceptions many of us live with.

Author Agnes Turnbull once said, "The mind, once suddenly aware of verity for the first time, immediately invents it again." This not only speaks to the pitfalls of interpretation, but also the problems of manipulation and omission. I feel it crucial for you to be aware of this otherwise, like most people, you will become a puppet bound by the persuading and prevailing impressions of the day. The truth will set you free.

Always ask questions. Always, always, always.

Diseases of Character

I can remember being as young as seven and walking down the street playing a game I called "plugs and outlets". I would imagine that half of my body was a series of plugs with retractable chords, and the other half was a series of outlets with flip-cover lids. I would also imagine that everyone I saw on the street was similarly configured.

The object of the game was to look for and initiate eye contact with people on the street. If I made any, I would "offer" a plug by giving a friendly face, to see if the person would allow me to "connect" with them. If they did, by returning a friendly face, that meant they opened their outlet and received my plug. Likewise, if people offered me a friendly face and I responded in kind, I was letting their plug into my outlet — we were connecting. At the end of each day, I would count how many connections I made.

I still play that game.

I make far fewer connections now, than I did as a child.

Earlier, when I was differentiating between ignorance and stupidity, I referred to the latter as a disease of character that will affect your reasoning and cripple your life. There are other such diseases equally injurious, but none more pernicious than greed and discrimination. They pose the greatest threat to the moral and ethical existence of thought and conduct. Because of them, no abomination or degradation of human behavior should ever be judged unlikely or impossible. If it can be conceived, it will be done.

Greed is quite blatant in its exhibition, so a brief caution should suffice. Please do not mistake the brevity for reduced consideration. Discrimination is more complex and can be more deceitfully deployed. It requires longer analysis. Both demand your utmost concern.

Greed is an excessive, egomaniacal desire to acquire, control, possess and consume beyond need or entitlement and without regard for consequence, even those threatening and damaging to self. I consider it even more baleful than discrimination, for greed will forsake all loyalties, whereas discrimination will at least preserve those of tribal allegiance.

Upon infecting, the first casualties of greed are those faculties of conscience humanity is most dependent on, compassion and sensibility. A line I once heard from a movie, while passing a television in a department store, underscores this point:

"You can't get people to act human,
if there is enough money involved."

Such is the case with greed. It discounts the value of everyone. To be diseased by it is to lose your soul, and to be without a soul is to be void of humane inclination. This is why drug dealers will peddle their poison to any ten year old, with the right amount of cash; and why gun merchants and arms dealers are willing to accommodate any patron, for their only concern is the profit of their transactions; and why the leaders of nations will starve and impoverish their people, for personal gain. They are the soulless, the greedy.

The best prevention is to boost your spiritual immunity, by continuously administering your compassion and inoculating your sensibility. If you understand that **compassion** is both the awareness and willingness to relieve the suffering of others, then you can protect your soul from callous disregard by acting accordingly. And if you comprehend **sensibility** to be the mental state from which sound reasoning produces practical judgment, you will not be defenseless against a mentality that debases yourself and everyone else.

Discrimination is the act or practice of discerning differences and effecting preferences. Accepting this, you can understand that some forms of discrimination are socially irrelevant, some are socially malevolent and others are socially redeeming. What distinguishes between them is whether they are rationally or irrationally derived and deployed.

For example, to say that you prefer the taste of white wine to red is a rational discrimination based upon an actual assessment of flavor. Relative to social interaction, it is meaningless, since no one is insulted, disadvantaged or violated by the preference. But to suggest that preference as being based solely on the color of the wine, without an actual assessment of flavor, is irrational.

Likewise, when parents teach their children to beware of "stranger danger", they are instructing a rational discrimination about assessing intention. It is socially redeeming, as it prescribes a safety consciousness for our most vulnerable. However, to instruct that a person is a danger simply because he/she is African-, Hispanic- or Arab-American, without an actual assessment of their intention, is irrational. After all, "prejudice" means "to prejudge".

Irrational discriminations are spawned by **skepticism**, the psychological discomfort of the unknown and the unfamiliar. They do not rely upon actual appraisal, assessment and experience, but rather are conjured mainly from emotion. Emotion requires no justification for its existence. It just needs to be felt.

People want their discomfort eased, so they create ideologies to make the unknown knowable and to fashion a familiarity for the unfamiliar. Since skepticism is willing to error on the side of disparagement for the sake of security, the process of demonization begins. Stereotypes and fallacies are formed and "rationalized" into generalities, for a reference guide. As that guide becomes formal and informal doctrine, a supplemental code of conduct is chartered to enforce it. An "-ism" is born. This process of derivation is the same, whether considering anti-Semitism, racism, sexism, classism or fascism.

However, since our first information about people comes from how we visually perceive them, this discomfort is often fear of one who appears different, "the other". As we seek survival within a social community, particularly a heterogeneous one, this fear of "the other" is key in the formation of our group or tribal identities. Survival's inclination is to equate "like body" with "like mind" and thus, "like intention". What looks similar is registered as what looks secure. Consequently, fear becomes scorn as condemnation of "the other" is encouraged and viewed as an essential emotion for survival.

The more disparate the differences, the greater the scorn. Such is the case with White v. Black racism, male v. female sexism and heterosexual v. homosexual dogmatism. The most intense scorn is **hate**, which I consider to be the maturation of fear. Consider this example for emphasis:

> A boy goes to a new school and knows no one there. At recess, he enters the playground wondering if he will find friendly reception from someone, only to become an obvious target for teasing and bullying. The aggression towards him conditions his fear. Daily, as he returns to the same harassment, his fear develops into anger about his treatment and resentment sets in. As weeks pass into months, his emotions ferment and he begins to fantasize a desirable and empowering solution, the elimination of his tormentors. His resentment develops into hate.

Fear is the "infant", resentment, the "adolescent" and hate, the "adult". With respect to discrimination, this is why the old instruct the young. Hate is adult fear.

Also understand that hate is an exorbitant emotion. The energy required to invest in, promote or sustain it is immense. So I urge you, with great warning, to never subsidize or underwrite its ambition. It can leave you morally bankrupt, impoverish your sense of humanity and rob your soul of its decency.

Though the consequences of hate are often blatant and well chronicled, one outcome seems to escape the perceptibility of those who seek to formulate it into an identity and a purpose. Hate has an internecine reality. It is a snake that will one day find its own tail appetizing. To devise, advocate and practice hate as a lifestyle is to guarantee self-destruction. This is true, regardless of the scope of examination. Whether viewing the global stage of Hitler, the national theater of the "Trench Coat Mafia", the local arena of Benjamin Smith or the psychological forum of suicidal terrorists, to hate is to insure your demise.

Often following the occurrence of hate crimes, religious and public officials appeal for tolerance. I appeal for you to consider such overtures futile, because I believe requests for tolerance are actually part of the problem, not the solution. Here is why.

Tolerance will never defeat bigotry, for tolerance just endures what is different. It does not eradicate the contagion of hate but instead renders it dormant, awaiting the conditions to become active. It does not prevent the judgments of inequality, or protect against the insults of suspicion or prescribe a remedy for disdain. As an antidotal behavior, tolerance is more placebo than cure.

The greater goal is **acceptance**, for it embraces our singular humanity while viewing what is different without malice or threat. It bolsters the immunity of appraising character and heals the wounds of violation. It thrives from the potential of interaction, rather than fear it as something to avoid. It promotes the fellowship of humane regard, rather than the diplomacy of civil segregation. As a curative mentality, acceptance is the ultimate antibody to hate.

The mentality of acceptance requires a transformation of the soul, not just a change in temperament. **"Change"** simply means to go from one phase to another. As the moon goes through phases it only changes appearance, not the substance of what it is. It is still the moon. Likewise, as years pass and decades change, hatred enters another phase. However, it still remains essentially what it is.

Dr. Martin Luther King, Jr. often cited this quote by Paul the Apostle: "Be ye transformed, by the renewal of your mind." Beyond any claim of wisdom assigned to one man or any denomination of faith declared on its behalf, the universal truth of these words is evident to anyone willing to see, rather than have their vision directed.

Transformation means to become totally other than, to undergo a process of alteration so profound, so dramatic, that the form altered from can never be recovered. As the caterpillar transforms into the butterfly, it can never recover its former self.

To reduce the presence and effects of discrimination, we must be transformed. Our spirit, our vision, our thoughts, our words, our deeds, our hearts, our emotions, our reasoning and our reasons, our motives and our motivations must be forever altered and deemed unrecoverable.

Since laws are made to guide conduct and not ordain thoughts, a mentality cannot be legislated. This is why racism still exists in America, despite the epic and heroic efforts of those during the Civil Rights activism of the 1950s and 1960s, which led to the Civil Rights Act of 1964. So in order to renew our minds, we must first rescue them from the dogma of insecurity that has been our imprisoning indoctrination from birth. Before there can be spiritual and behavioral transformation, there must first be mental and emotional reclamation. If we take back the purity of our hearts, the childlike purity that existed long before the contamination of adult fears, we can do this, for the essence of a child is to be free from the infection of lies. Only the heart of a child can make new, again.

Reclamation is only possible if we elect to investigate for, educate with, pursue and promote truth. Please remember this, live it and encourage it in others.

If that transformation is to ever be realized on a grand social level, the paradigms that have constructed our society must be dramatically and profoundly altered. If you can reason this and are impassioned about actively assisting that process of alteration, you must recognize this crucial point. I firmly believe, with the greatest attestation of conviction, that:

> The moral and social evolution of humanity will never equal the marvel and magnitude of our physical evolution, until women have attained the equal status in society they desire, deserve and are entitled to.

Women constitute half of all humanity. **Half**. It is totally irrational and inconceivable to think, that as a species we can develop to our highest form, realize our pinnacle achievement and execute our ultimate good while discounting, suppressing and ignoring half of who we are.

Cultures around the world verify this truth, with shameless dishonor. Those societies and nations who demonstrate the most repressive, contemptuous and degrading regard for their women are amongst the most unstable, the most impoverished, the most politically abusive, the most socially archaic, the most technologically inept and the most morally debased environments in existence.

I could follow that observation with a rather lengthy dissertation about the contributions of women in history, or the differences in gender orientation that direct differences in behavior or the drawbacks of exclusionary policies for anyone in society, but they are not necessary to make this point. It really is that simple. If we want the full actualization of our humanity, which will effect the social transformation of our interaction with one another, women must be included, involved and deemed invaluable to that aim. To whatever degree you can assist that objective, I urge you to do so.

You must also challenge within, if you are to forever alter your society. Understand "within" to not only mean self-examination and accountability, but also the questioning, contesting and denouncing of discrimination within your sphere of influence. Until European Americans challenge other European Americans and African Americans challenge other African Americans about the racial myopia and mythology both adhere to, racism will always influence how the two groups deal with one another. Likewise with Jews to other Jews, Muslims to other Muslims, men to other men, women to other women.

Should you challenge for transformation, you will most certainly encounter alienation and resentment. But do not fear nor be deterred by the opinions and reactions of others. As the light of a flickering flame attracts the moth, so to does challenge attract hostility. But like the moth's failure to recognize the consumptive power of the flame, so to will the wrath of your detractors be charred by your conviction. Keep the fire of your effort kindled and their hostility will be consumed by your results. Stoke the passion of your determination with **courage:** the ability to act when confronted by fear.

Hostility creates enemies. My analysis of history suggests that there are four ways to deal with them: distance, détente, deterrence, destruction. Of the four, deterrence is the most advised. Be of such power within as to dissuade the invitation of destruction, to direct the discourse of détente and to warrant the distancing by those of ill will.

In your pursuits, always remember to employ civility. Its practice seems to be a lost conduct in our society. To insure that it will always align your demeanor, I ask you to adopt this definition, one given to me years ago by a man from the Philippines:

Civility is the lubrication of society.
Those who fail to learn this are destined to produce friction.

Early on in life, my mother encouraged and insisted that I interact and engage with children and people of other races and cultures, on all levels: in education, in sports, in the workplace, in friendship, in romance. She felt it was not enough to tell me that I was equal to everyone, but that I had to experience it to truly believe it. As she would say, "You have to live it, to know it." I only wish every parent gave their child the same instruction.

Joan was also fond of saying, "The best way to beat stupidity is with intelligence. Attack with what you know." So I felt I had to thoroughly understand social discrimination, if I was going to beat it.

When I was fifteen, I began seriously thinking about the problem. I reasoned that everyone on earth fell into two categories of bias: racism and sexism. We are all of some racial designation and we are all of some gender or sexuality distinction. In my youthful naiveté, I imagined that if I could figure out the origins of sexism and racism, I could share my discovery with others. Then maybe I could help facilitate an understanding that would decrease or stop our investment, in these forms of discrimination. Then everyone could really live in peace.

Though lofty and idealistic, I was convinced of the simplicity of my reasoning, so I began investigating the root cause of bigotry. On my first day at the library for this noble endeavor, I read something that deeply impressed me. I came upon it by chance, just flipping through a book of quotes. I liked it so much, that I wrote it down. It was attributed to the distinguished American educator, Horace Mann:

"Be ashamed to die, until you have
won some victory for humanity."

Inspired by those words, I decided to make defeating discrimination my attempt at victory. I hope to convince you to accept the same task.

Though I have been concerned with examining and deconstructing all forms of discrimination, undermining racism has dominated my efforts. To that end, my focus and actions have been guided by how I define it:

> **Racism** is a belief that mental, intellectual, psychological, emotional, behavioral and moral differences between people can be directly attributed to differences in physical appearance, particularly skin color. Additionally, racism is the social, political and economic cause-and-effect created by projecting that belief into social interaction.

The latter part of that definition has mistakenly led many who are disenfranchised by racism into believing, that they and the group to which they are identified with cannot be racists. This thinking exist because those who feel this way contend, that the label of being a "racist" only applies to those who socially, politically and economically benefit from racism. I have heard many an African American espouse this view, despite professing bigotry towards Hispanics, Asians and Arabs, as well as European Americans.

Understand that such thinking is codependent to the reasons racism continues, because it sanctions a point of view that the reactionary sentiment of bitterness, triggered by being the recipient of bigotry, makes counter discrimination a moral entitlement. I can certainly testify to the truth that being treated as "less than" produces anger, even rage, both of which can be easily converted into an "anti-" mentality against those who incite these emotions. But whether assertion or rebuttal, racism is racism. To fashion a blanket contempt against an entire group of people, regardless of reason, without reckoning the character of the individual is still discrimination.

To hold this point of view, whether you benefit from or are disadvantaged by racism, means to internalize aversion as a component of who you are. If you are on the receiving end of prejudice, this only subsidizes the existence of the very mentality that threatens you. Furthermore, it causes you to overemphasize that aspect of yourself that is being targeted as an alienating distinction. In other words, why play the color game when you neither invented it, nor are able to dictate the rules by which it is being played?

This underscores my perspective about constructing identity. The components of your physical being, whether you are tall or short, fat or thin, brown or cream in complexion are all bricks in the pyramid of being human. Neither is the sole or primary determinant of anyone's humanity. Thus, to define others or yourself principally by one component of self, especially a physical attribute, means to reduce the value of being human. No less than Dr. King reasoned the outcome of this, when he suggested that to reduce the humanity of one, reduces the humanity of all.

I contend that once African Americans grasp that we need to define ourselves beyond our color, we will thoroughly realize and utilize the awesome power of being fully human. Then and only then will we overcome. It is an egregious insult to our ancestors that we have yet to realize this, for they overcame slavery. Nothing in our present or future, as a people beset by bias, will ever be more challenging than that.

The same is true for women and gender, relative to sexism and homosexuals and sexuality, relative to heterosexism. The effort must be made to define self and perceive others as fully human.

Keep this in mind, for the time will come when you must challenge the seduction of such emotions that would tempt you to discriminate. Everyone must confront such a moment.

Over the years, I have also reasoned that perhaps the greatest difficulty in debunking discrimination is that its emotional base supports a multilevel phenomenon. For example, racism exists in various forms and to varying degrees. My perspective has been to stratify it along four principle gradations: racially conditioned, racially reactive, racially virulent and racially benign.

In America, everyone is **racially conditioned**, whether born from generations of established citizenship or a newly arrived immigrant. We are all indoctrinated to formulate, assign and accept character judgments based solely on physical differences, particularly skin color. This is an unavoidable socialization instructed in ways both intentional and inadvertent, blatant and covert. It has been woven into the fabric of American culture, from the inception of our nationhood.

The next shade is defined as those who are **racially reactive**. These are people whose behavior is guided by the propaganda of stereotypes assigned to physical differences. This is the most predominant, problematic and consequential of the gradations, because its pervasiveness provides a veneer of validity many are convinced by. People of this distinction have a definite awareness and knowledge of racism. However, they either feel their prejudices reflect a practical sensibility or do not characterize them as being morally repugnant, because everyone else projects similar biases. This speaks more to a conduct directed by stigma, rather than a discomfort triggered by differences. Consequently, it enables the conviction and commitment to discrimination that allows it to become casually, formally and institutionally promoted and practiced.

The next shade defines the group most focused upon, those who are **racially virulent**. They are a small but conspicuous segment of the population, due to the vitriolic sensationalism in their words and deeds. Like clothes used to cover the self-consciousness of nakedness, they suit up in an armor of antipathy, to guard the enormity of their insecurity. With a xenophobic distortion that warps all logic and lucidity, they condemn, avoid, reject and in some cases, desire and seek the elimination of "the other", to effect racial inoculation and preservation.

Finally, the true minority, those who are **racially benign**. Either by virtue of their innate being or by an acquired capacity for rational scrutiny, these are people who have never invested in or have reasoned out of their racial conditioning. Despite an awareness of racism and perhaps even personal experiences with it, they are not jaded or persuaded by prejudice. Their assessment of people is truly one of character appraisal based upon objective, individual interaction. They assign no premium or discount to physical differences.

These gradations apply to all people, regardless of skin color. Hopefully, you will find them useful when gauging the behavior of others. Additionally, I desire them to motivate your internal audit for any investment in discrimination. To be racially benign is the hue I wish your mind and heart to be.

Despite my efforts against discrimination, racism is a malignancy I continue to deal with daily: from the wary glances of those who pass by me on the street; from the women who clutch their purses and their children as I near them; from police officers who only look at me with criminal assessment; from store personnel never willing to greet or assist, yet eager to survey my every move; from the fixed gazes of avoidance by those who can only interpret my presence as an encounter to survive, rather than an innocuous experience. The psychic assault is unending.

You have already experienced racism. I know this because of a playground incident you conveyed to me at age five. I wrote you a poem to overcome it. Though you are biracial, yours is not the pale skin that would otherwise conceal you from judgment. Even before your birth, I had concerns about how you would interpret yourself from your skin. That concern became a reality, when you were three and a half years old.

It was at that age, you asked me when you were going to turn dark brown like me. I tried to explain that your skin color was a beautiful shade and might never get darker, because just as everyone has their own name, they also have their own color. You did not find this to be an acceptable explanation. The thought of not getting darker was so distressing, you cried for nearly twenty minutes. And for the next four weeks, you campaigned and lobbied to anyone who would listen, that one day you were going to turn dark brown.

At first I was humored by your behavior, but I soon realized it was a serious issue for you. I found myself a bit unnerved, confronted by my first experience of racial affirmation for my child.

I knew I had to do something to help you reconcile your color identity. I became convinced that whatever it was, had to be physically demonstrable. I reasoned this because a child's world is far more literal than it is conceptual. I had to show you a solution, not just tell you one.

One Saturday, I took you on a field trip, the purpose of which was to engrave you with a positive association of the many shades of "brown" that exist. Being that racism is a complex issue dealing with color, I reasoned that a singular focus on color would be a simple beginning.

We visited three candy stores, three furniture stores and three fur salons. At every candy store I had you pick a piece of chocolate, each different in size, taste and shade. You ate and enjoyed them. After each sampling, I would ask you to tell me the color of the candy, to which you would simply answer, "Brown." Next we went to the furniture stores, where I had you select your favorite table, each of a different style and wood type. Again, after every selection I would ask for their colors and you responded, "Brown". Finally, we visited the fur salons, where I had you touch three different furs. You were fascinated by their textures. Once more you were asked their colors and once more you answered, "Brown."

On the train ride home, we discussed the outing. I reminded you of the wonderful "brown" things you experienced and how they tasted, looked and felt. Afterwards, you sat on my lap in silence. I did not press you any further, choosing instead to allow some time to gauge if you had processed the experience, as I had hoped. Shortly before arriving at our stop, you turned to me and said, "Brown is a nice color. I like brown." So far, my plan was working.

When we got home, I directed you to the kitchen. I told you I was going to teach you how to make a cup of cappuccino. You were familiar with the term, for one of the first nicknames your mother gave you was "The Cappuccino Bambino". I placed on a plate a scoop of ground coffee, a pinch of cinnamon, a teaspoon of sugar and a small glass of milk. I then suggested that you pretend the coffee and the cinnamon were me and that the sugar and milk were your mother. I explained that when we mixed them all together, we would make "you".

I poured brewed coffee into a glass mug and instructed you to add the steamed milk, until the coffee's color matched the shade of your skin. It took some time, but when you blended the right shade, you smiled and laughed. After adding the sugar and cinnamon and letting it cool, you tasted it. You responded, "I like me a lot. I taste good." I was satisfied you interpreted the meaning of the cappuccino.

Know that every time you look in the mirror, you see the evidence of humanity's harmony in your biracial, multiethnic composition, a harmony that convincingly refutes the fraudulence of racial superiority, inferiority and incompatibility. Just you being you is greater than any argument anyone can make against the absurdity of discrimination, for your physical being exists without self-conflict.

Also know that the terms "Black" and "White", as they are used to describe a person or a people, are political terms employed for social convenience and expedience. Physically speaking, (with some exceptions like scarring, severe burns, albinism, prolonged sun exposure, etc.), people are neither white nor black. Furthermore, a scan of any heterogeneous environment will reveal that "Blacks" and "Whites" come in varied hues and shades, sometimes to the point of racial confusion.

Neither do these terms have any basis in nationhood or geography. Whereas "Irish-" or "Polish-", used as prefixes to "American", are national and geographic references to Ireland and Poland, "Black-" or "White-" are references to a social, bureaucratic appraisal of people. This is why people can be referred to as "acting white" or "acting black". There exist no country anywhere identified by name, in whole or in part, as "White" or "Black". So these terms must be seen and recognized for what they are — the determinants of division.

Their use as a reference to people is unavoidable in this country and the world, for the politics of race is not unique to America. However, if you recognize the essence and intent of these terms, you will more likely employ them in your examination of the division they serve, rather than unwittingly use them to facilitate the politicization of your identity and existence, as well as the identity and existence of others.

A quote by the Danish theologian and philosopher Soren Kierkegaard holds that, "Once you label me, you negate me." The significance of this cannot be understated, for history is clear in its record and instruction. To politicize the identity and existence of a person or a people often equates with an effort to dehumanize them. Your racial duality means that many more attempts will be made to politicize who you are. Though racial designations and affiliations are unavoidable, do not become nullified or trapped by them.

Never accept any reduction, suppression or denial of your total being. It is far more important to discover, determine and invest in your human identity, than in any racial identity assigned to or chosen by you. As I stated before, "race" is a component of your total humanity. Don't just realize a part of what you are. Actualize all of who you are.

Unfortunately, one of the greatest ironies of human behavior is the ability to recognize and comprehend the injurious consequences of our actions, and yet remain motivated to recreate the conduct of ill effect. Our failure or refusal to learn, acknowledge and accept the lessons of bigotry means we will continue to relive its outcome. And so the politics of race continues.

Fortunately, you live in an era in which scientific exploration into the genetic secrets that makes us who we are is unprecedented. So far, recent discoveries have completely undermined the notion of "race" and a racial hierarchy. It has already been determined that the genetic composition of every human being on Earth is more than 99% identical. Furthermore, only a **.012%** difference in our entire gene code determines the differences we assign to "race". A similar differential is thought to represent what determines shoe size.

I learned that truth, while reading the November 1994 issue of Discover magazine. This proves that the information is out there in mainstream newspapers, books and magazines, available for anyone willing to see. Don't just take my word for it. Endeavor to research on your own. That way you will not doubt or discount my findings, but rather be convinced by your own pursuit.

Maybe one day the scientific model of a "mitochondrial Eve" will succeed the religious tenet of the "biblical Eve", as the dominant belief of the world's people. Perhaps then we will have a greater understanding of our common lineage. Then maybe the collective family of humanity will realize the falsity of the racial classifications, proposed and advanced by Carolus Linneaus and Johann Blumenbach. Then we could develop a resistance to the dogma of racial insecurity, by vaccinating ourselves with an understanding of our universal likeness.

Then, perhaps our nation's fixation on labeling its citizenry would become a societal relic for future generations to examine, rather than a social practice our present generation still engages in. And finally, maybe then we would all be able to look at the mosaic of our country and see "Americans", rather than racial tribes whose place in society is determined by the prefix assigned to them.

Maybe.

My Final Instruction

IF

If you can keep your head when all about you
Are losing theirs and blaming it on you;
If you can trust yourself when all men doubt you,
But make allowance for their doubting too;
If you can wait and not be tired by waiting,
Or being lied about, don't deal in lies;
Or being hated, don't give way to hating,
And yet don't look too good, nor talk to wise.

If you can dream and not make dreams your master,
If you can think and not make thoughts your aim;
If you can meet with Triumph and Disaster
And treat those two impostors just the same;
If you can bear to hear the truth you've spoken,
Twisted by knaves to make a trap for fools,
Or watch the things you gave your life to, broken,
And stoop to build 'em up with worn out tools.

If you can make one heap of all your winnings
And risk it on one turn of pitch-and-toss,
And lose and start again at your beginnings,
And never breathe a word about your loss;
If you can force your heart and nerve and sinew,
To serve your turn long after they are gone,
And hold on when there is nothing in you,
Except the Will which says to them, "Hold on!"

If you can walk with crowds and keep your virtue,
Or walk with kings, nor lose the common touch;
If neither foes nor loving friends can hurt you,
If all men count with you, but none too much;
If you can fill the unforgiving minute
With sixty-seconds worth of distance run —
Yours is the earth and everything that's in it,
And which is more, you'll be a Man, my son!

— Rudyard Kipling

I gave you that poem when you were eight years old and asked you to keep it, so one day you could learn and understand it. Make it your creed and you will live as I have always dreamed and hoped you would.

There. I have written what both duty and love have directed. Given my proclivity, I could have authored much more. I restrained myself for two reasons. One, to leave space for your own rumination. Two, because one day I hope to have conversations with you again. So in conclusion, I leave this parting reflection.

There are moments throughout everyday, when a lull in activity or a recess in concentration is encroached upon, by images and memories of a past insistent about being remembered. Those recollections are always there, standing in line like a multitude of hungry, waiting and hoping to be served. Sometimes their numbers are overwhelming, making the task to tend to them seemingly impossible. Other times a fixation on one provides a lingering moment of consideration, a chance to feel connected to a history that cannot be forgotten. In those moments, you are always there.

Ambivalence is also companion to those occasions, for what is sweet in the recovery of memory is often bitter in the realization of the present. When that present exceeds its allowance for grief, I seek relief from music. What cannot be felt or expressed in written or spoken words can often be conveyed in a melody, or a rhythm or a lyric sung.

When I seek such relief, my music of choice is the one true art form America invented. Jazz gives me this conveyance, for it was born of a people who have always provided in song what was lacking, needed or wanting in their lives. If you listen to Ellington, Bassie, Miles, Marsalis, Monk, Tyner, Holiday or Fitzgerald, you might also find the relief I speak of.

What I have written is meant to express the greatest of concern, hope and love I have for you. The future will answer whether you found it useful and were motivated back to me. But in case our destinies are not destined, I propose a song of lasting sentiment. A collaboration between Arte Butler and Phyllis Molinary yields an empathy that serves my emotions well. I recall its verses or listen to it, whenever I think of the possibility of life without you. It helps sedate that misgiving.

I prefer the version sung by Shirley Horn on the CD entitled, A Tribute To Oscar Peterson. The song:

"Here's To Life"

I remember the day, I taught you the word "infinity". You were one month past your fifth birthday. We were walking home from the park with your uncle, after playing softball. You were sitting on my shoulders, as I carried you down the street.

While on top, you began playfully questioning how much I loved you, an exchange many parents have with their children. You repeatedly asked, "This much?", as you incrementally moved your hands further and further apart. Each time I answered, "Bigger."

When you could not spread your arms any wider, I told you to hold your finger in the air and notice where it started and stop. I explained that in order to measure something it had to have a beginning and an end, like the beginning and end of your finger.

Then I asked you to find the beginning and the end of the sky. You said you couldn't. I suggested that the reason you were unable to was because the sky had no beginning or end. That's when I told you that "infinity" was the measurement for something with no beginning or end.

Upon hearing it, you liked the word a lot and began repeating it several times. By now, we were steps away from the building you lived in. As I lifted you from my shoulders, hugged and kissed you, I told you that my love for you was like the sky — as big as infinity.

Whenever you need to know "How much?", just look up for the answer.

I Love You,
Papa

May 26, 2000

About The Author

Michael Tyler grew up in Chatam Village, on the southside of Chicago, the third son of four siblings.

Reared by a mother rich in love and commitment, he completed college and went on to become a fitness consultant.

In time, he fulfilled his greatest ambition by becoming a father. And with that distinction, he esteems the value of all children by the hopeful promise of redemption and renewal inherent within them.

His guiding principle in life:

"Be ashamed to die, until you have won some victory for humanity."
— Horace Mann

Tyler continues to reside in Chicago with his loving wife, Julie and their remarkable son, Ziggi.

NOTES

NOTES

NOTES

NOTES

NOTES

NOTES

NOTES

NOTES

NOTES

NOTES

NOTES

NOTES

NOTES

NOTES

NOTES

NOTES

NOTES

NOTES

Printed in the United States
1113900003B

9 781403 356987